W9-ADH-746

Praise for Janet Sternburg

Phantom Limb

Janet Sternburg has found the perfect metaphor for the tragedy of pain and loss, the ultimate inevitabilities of life.

BILL MOYERS

At a time when many people are writing and publishing memoirs, Sternburg's *Phantom Limb* is uncommon. The book is a meditation on memory. The author experiences difficulties and writes about them, but she does so without a sense of victimhood or self-pity. Instead, she tells a tender story of the expansiveness of love.

THE JEWISH WEEK

Feelings shared by countless others ... luminously detailed recollections ... moments of consoling happiness.

KIRKUS

...part moving account of greater love in the face of her mother's approaching death, part medical inquiry into neurology, and part spiritual meditation on the struggles and sufferings that living visits on each of us. Sternburg shows that emotional and spiritual integration is possible ...

BOOKLIST

Sternburg's prose is powered by imagistic accuracy and psychological immediacy—two horses that lesser writers let run wild. She holds their reins in a firm hand, and gently guides this book with intelligence and humility.

LIANA HOLMBERG, Author of *Manoa*

Optic Nerve: Photopoems

These carefully wrought poems are the perfect analogues to Sternburg's superb photographs: they are spare and direct yet oddly mysterious, and their everyday language is charged with emotion, energy, and good humor ... Sternburg maintains an exquisite poise.

> MARJORIE PERLOFF, Author of *Poetry in a New Key* and *The Vienna Paradox: A Memoir*

[Janet Sternburg's] photopoems open up new ideas of metaphor, redefining both poetry and photography with a sense of interplay that can only come with equally weighted ability.

> MOLLY PEACOCK, Author of *The Paper Garden: Mrs. Delany Begins Her Life's Work at 72*

Success in more than one artistic medium is a talent all in itself; one that has been accomplished with an economy of grace and fortitude in Janet Sternburg's collection *Optic Nerve: Photopoems*.

> MARIE LECRIVAIN, Author of *Poetic Diversity*

The Writer On Her Work, Volume One

Groundbreaking ... a landmark.

> POETS & WRITERS MAGAZINE

The Writer on Her Work is a collection which belongs on many reading lists, beside the bed, in the library, alongside the desk, in the classroom, in the bag that holds the notebooks and manuscripts.

> ADRIENNE RICH, Author of *A Human Eye*

I don't remember exactly how I happened upon Sternburg's *The Writer on Her Work*. It seems now that it was always there, on the bookshelf next to my desk, where I keep the touchstone books. As I read of other women's struggles with their families, their traditions, their fears—all summed up on that blank sheet of paper, I felt like Molly Bloom at the end of James Joyce's *Ulysses*, turning pages rapidly, saying, Yes, oh yes, yes indeed, uhhum, ay si ... I was not alone.

> JULIA ALVAREZ, Author of *Return to Sender*

A compelling and superbly crafted collection ... It speaks to the active creative spirit.

> PHILADELPHIA INQUIRER

Tough, humorous, graceful, caring and joyful.

> WASHINGTON POST

The Writer On Her Work, Volume Two

This book is a gift in every possible way.

CAROLYN SEE, *The Los Angeles Times*

These books belongs in the library of every woman who wants to make art.

500 GREAT BOOKS BY WOMEN

Copyright ©2014
Janet Sternburg

All rights reserved. No part
of this book may be repro-
duced in any form or by any
electronic or mechanical
means, including informa-
tion storage-and-retrieval
systems, without prior per-
mission in writing from the
Publisher, except for brief
quotations embodied in
critical articles and reviews.

Library of Congress
Cataloging-in-Publication Data

Sternburg, Janet.
White matter : a memoir of family
and medicine / Janet Sternburg.
pages cm
ISBN 978-0-9893604-9-4
1. Sternburg, Janet-Family-
    Health.
2. Frontal lobotomy-Patients-
    United States-Biography.
3. Frontal lobotomy-History.
4. Psychosurgery-History.

I. Title.
RD594.S744 2015
617.4'81-dc23
[B]
2014020100

Hawthorne Books
& Literary Arts

9   2201 Northeast 23rd Avenue
8   3rd Floor
7   Portland, Oregon 97212
6   hawthornebooks.com
5   *Form*:
4   Adam McIsaac/Sibley House
3   Printed in China
2   Set in Paperback

for
Herman Engel
Etta Somerset
as always, for Steve

White Matter

A Memoir of Family
and Medicine
Janet Sternburg

HAWTHORNE BOOKS & LITERARY ARTS
Portland, Oregon | MMXV

There is no pain. Suddenly, while you're asleep, they'll absorb your minds, your memories, and you're reborn into an untroubled world . . .

— *INVASION OF THE BODY SNATCHERS*

Hello,
Is there anybody in there
Just nod if you can hear me
Is there anyone at home

—PINK FLOYD, "COMFORTABLY NUMB"

To feel is a fact.

—CLARICE LISPECTOR

The Family

IDA SMALL
(b. unknown, Byelorussia; SMALNITSKY changed to SMALL at Ellis Island)
marries
PHILIP GOLDSTEIN (b. unknown, Poland)

Their children (b. Boston), in order of birth starting from eldest

MINNA b. 1904
marries SAM   Son DAN b. 1930

JEN b. 1905
Unmarried

BENNIE b. 1909
Unmarried

HELEN b. 1911
marries LOU   Daughter JANET b. 1943

PAULINE b. 1914
marries GEORGE   Son PHIL b. 1939

FRANCIE b. 1920
marries HARRY

THIS IS THE STORY OF A FAMILY WHO MADE MISTAKES. Who made choices based on imperfect knowledge—of the world, and of themselves—and had to live with their consequences, as did I, the next generation of that family.

The words "prefrontal lobotomy" were spoken often, common currency growing up in my family. Sometimes I'd hear the term shortened to "frontal" lobotomy. I had no idea what *pre*-meant, but it seemed to confer authority, as though the speaker knew what he was talking about. This childhood recognition of distinctions made me—a Jewish, lower-middle-class child—a true citizen of Boston, a city that prided itself on being correct. I really should not have heard any of those words.

By the time I was born, my uncle, my mother's brother, had already undergone a prefrontal lobotomy. My aunt, my mother's sister, was lobotomized more than a decade later. These events, these people I grew up with, seemed an ordinary part of my life. A child says to herself, "This is how they were, this is how they had to be." Later, an adult questions whether anything *has* to be.

"In one family? Your uncle and your aunt?"

A friend asked me this some years ago, unable to believe I grew up taking for granted two lobotomized relatives as part of my everyday life. I'd mentioned this casually to her—only a parenthesis in another story—but she was aghast.

"Your mother was one of six siblings?" She did the division: "One third of her family?"

My friend had heard about lobotomies; many in my generation had read Ken Kesey's novel *One Flew Over the Cuckoo's Nest*,
with its portrayal of lobotomy as a surgical punishment for speaking out against authority. But she'd never heard of anyone with two
lobotomized relatives. She looked at me strangely, trying to comprehend how I could have failed to realize that something horrify-
ing had happened in my own family.

When I was no longer a word-crazy child in Boston, no longer a naïve young woman in New York but instead an adult, living in California, secure and happy, only then did the so-called
ordinary return as mystery. The years came back to me when my
aunt and uncle were driven to our house, my uncle in a corduroy
car coat like the ones my father and other uncles wore, my aunt
dolled up by her other sisters, her hair Spray-Netted stiff. They
were greeted; they sat blankly on the couch—Bennie at one end
virtually unmoving, my aunt crumpled into the far corner—while
my mother made dinner, my aunt brought over a Bundt cake, my
father and uncles played cards, all of them through the years suc-
ceeding, or failing, or something in between.

With the sharp return of memories came the realization that
even as a child I had a slight awareness, compounded from fear
and pity, that something wrong had been done, that it couldn't be
right for people to be this way, expressionless and indifferent to
anything around them. But on the surface I saw my mother and
aunts as they saw themselves—good, kind people who went out
of their way to help others—to drive the widow home, to drop in
on the old and lonely childless couple who lived downstairs. Now I
asked, "If my relatives had been so good and kind, how could they
have done this to their siblings? Especially the second lobotomy,
when they'd seen the consequences of the first?" My questions
grew, encompassing my family and more: What converges—our
selves, our histories, our knowledge, imperfect as it may be—as
we come up against the great difficulties that ask us to make decisions? And how do we live with the decisions we make?

I began with research, getting a kick out of finding movies in which lobotomy makes a surreptitious appearance, perhaps most obviously in *Planet of the Apes* when Charlton Heston sees a scar on the forehead of his unresponsive friend and wheels around to accuse his ape captors: "You did this to him! You've removed his frontal lobes." Or, less overt, in *I Walked with a Zombie* when a doctor diagnoses a character's zombified condition as the result of a fever in her frontal lobes: "I prefer to think of her as a sleepwalker who can never be awakened—feeling nothing, knowing nothing." Then I went on a long reading excursion into what I thought of as Famous Relatives of The Lobotomized, among them Allen Ginsberg (his mother) and Tennessee Williams (his sister), their stories transformed into "Kaddish" and *The Glass Menagerie*. I spent a long period reading up on findings in neurobiology, then made a dip into philosophy to read about the problem of evil. Then I faced it: all this research, while compelling and an intrinsic part of the story, was also a way for me to stay at a safe distance from the implications of what was close to me.

It wasn't possible to stay at that distance; everything I learned brought my own story near. When I read about what happened before a lobotomy, I saw my aunt's shaven head. When I found out about what happened during the surgery, it was my uncle Bennie's brain I pictured, his frontal lobes disconnected. When I read about people submitting their relatives to lobotomy, I understood. It was my own family I needed to speak with.

But only one was left.

I.

I.

2002

I WAIT IN THE LIBRARY OF PAULINE'S ASSISTED LIVING residence. Newspapers drape over a wooden rack; a gas fire burns politely. Residents are reading in wing chairs, women wearing pearls, a single strand each, men with a natty look of willed self-respect, jackets sporting the elbow patches of former academics. Ordinarily I'd be on the first plane out of Boston after my reading, glad to be winging back to California where the past casts no shadows, away from the stories that my mother and aunts poured into me while I—a preternaturally interested child—was soaking up material for the books I'd write from the perspective of middle-age.

Instead I've driven out to a western suburb through an old scuffed landscape, teeth gritted, to visit the last aunt. I haven't seen Pauline in years, and I'm not at all sure how I feel about it now. But there's no time to reflect—the elevator door opens and there she is, gray hair coiled in an immaculate French twist, navy suit and crisp white blouse; her pillar-of-the-community look. She stops, calls my name, and opens her arms wide.

I step into her embrace and out of it—perhaps too quickly.

"Can I possibly tell you," she says, "how much it means to me to have you back in my life?"

I have had my reasons for staying away.

Eager for me to see her apartment, Pauline takes me along a corridor, her gait brisk, past low sideboards with sprays of artificial orchids in majolica vases. On a shelf beside her door, Pauline has placed a bowl of Hershey's Kisses, on offer to passersby. I unwrap the silver foil, eat one Kiss and pocket two more, nervous and irritated to recognize in myself a vestigial desire to impress my aunt—to show this person whose approval I should no longer care about that I too have risen in the world.

On a low bench set under the windows Pauline has displayed her prized possession, an elaborate dollhouse she and her husband made together, a replica of the house where they'd once lived. In its master bedroom, Pauline has turned a scrap of flowered chintz into a canopy for a four-poster bed; in the corner of the living room, the lid of a piano remains perpetually propped open. On her coffee table are the latest books for her book club—Amos Oz's latest novel, Alice Munro's stories—and the books written by us, the cousins: Dan, a novelist; Pauline's son, a historian; and myself, a writer of memoir. The five sisters of my mother's family didn't turn out many children, but they were prolific in giving birth to words; in my generation, three of the four of us are writers.

Pauline goes to the kitchen and opens a cupboard, asking what kind of tea I'd like. This is the moment to ask the question I've brought with me: "What was wrong with all of you?" But there's no way that I can ask that directly, so I introduce the subject with another question that I hope she'll find flattering.

"Isn't it strange," I say. "So many people in our family are brilliant—look at you. And yet we've had so much mental illness? Look at Bennie … "

Pauline slides the kettle over to an unlit burner as though putting it on hold and ignites with the passion of a lifetime.

"My sisters lied," she says. "My brother was not insane. Bennie was lied about day and night."

She slides the kettle back to the heat, where it begins to whistle.

"Pauline," I say, "he was schizophrenic."

I watch as she struggles to lift the kettle, take it from her and pour with my own unsteady hand. Pauline has overturned everything I've believed all my life.

I take a sip of the tea, so hot it burns my tongue. Good—it keeps me from saying what I want to say.

"Bennie was never the way my sisters made him out to be. I knew my brother for who he was, we played together for years. He never lost touch with reality."

"Why would anyone lie about him?"

"It was my sister Minna. She encouraged my other sisters to say terrible things about Bennie. They all went along with her."

Pauline must have seen disbelief written across my face.

"I know, Minna was your special friend. She understood you, she encouraged you. You needed someone who could give you a different perspective from your parents who—I hate to say this, but it's true—were very limited people."

Inside I recoil at her accusations of Minna, and now this jab at my parents cloaked in sympathy for me but diminishing them nonetheless. Yes, they were limited in some ways, but we all are. And besides, their lives had dignity and it's not for Pauline to take it away.

"Minna had it in for me because Leon, her so-called great love, liked me too much."

Pauline is going on while I figure out the years since she and Minna had competed for Leon's attention, more than sixty...

"I never thought Bennie should have had the lobotomy," she says. "He would have grown out of it."

"He couldn't have grown out of it, Pauline," I say. "He tried to kill people."

"That's what you grew up hearing. They all lied."

I can't go on. It's awful. I manage to divert her attention, ask about her son and his family, what she thinks of the books she has been reading, anything that gets her off track.

It's time for me to leave. She hands me a parting gift, a little china shoe that suggests something a Fragonard woman on a swing might wear. I don't care for its pastel rosettes, or for its evidence of Pauline's will to miniaturize. Besides it would always remind me of this crazy conversation. I try to come up with a reason not to take it: "It will break, Pauline. I'm going all the way to California."

From a drawer of neatly rolled up stockings, Pauline takes out a black velvet pouch, folding it back to show me that it's lined with white satin quilting. She inserts the shoe.

"It will be safe," she says, drawing the strings tight. "When you look at it, remember me."

ON THE WAY out I stop by her door and pocket a handful of chocolate Kisses. I walk through the hushed library and out of the residence, its buildings painted white with black shutters conjuring a New England town arrayed around a perfectly tended ersatz village green. I cross over toward my car, stepping on the grass as I go.

In the parking lot I stand still, appalled at what she has just told me. What shall I do about her accusations?

My first inclination is to let sleeping dogs do what they're supposed to—stay narcotized, even if they're twitching with bad dreams.

Would there be a way for me to get at the truth? If I were to try, I'd have to begin by going back to a time before I was born. I'd have to rely on stories told to me by my mother and other aunts, especially Minna, herself suspect in Pauline's view. And I'd have to supplement them with my imagination, which I'd hope would be scrupulous—as close as possible to the stories as I've heard them—but which would inevitably lean toward fiction.

Pauline, though, is intelligent and seductive.

Insidious, too, with her aura of certainty.

What if there were truth in what she said?

What if I've been living with an illusion of goodness and kindness? What if everything was different from what I'd believed?

My first thought—to let sleeping dogs do what they're supposed to do?

Ha! Impossible. Dogs don't stay asleep.

Time to get up, sniff, go back, bark.

2.

Front row: Bennie, Pauline, Helen (my mother) *Back row*: Minna, Philip (their father), Jen

IT IS ALMOST ONE HUNDRED YEARS SINCE MY MOTHER and her siblings were born in the first decades of twentieth century America.

This is their ur-portrait. The earliest. The original. The one that all the sisters had on their walls. The one that I too have, although I keep mine in a shoebox jumbled with other old photographs. For them, it was an image of the earthly paradise that had once, for a brief time, been family.

On that bright day in 1915, my grandfather posed for a family portrait, proud to be surrounded by his children on an outing in Roxbury's Franklin Park, one of the jewels in Olmstead's Emerald Necklace adorning Boston. Earlier, the family had passed through a formal entrance called The Greeting, a democratic gesture of welcome that had special meaning to the mostly immigrant neighborhood. The children had thrown peanuts into the elephant enclosure, inhaled the pungent smell of cracked shells and elephant urine. I know those smells because many decades later I too grew up in Roxbury, an only child who went to those same cages with peanuts I'd push through openings in the chainlink fence. Then though, posing for the photograph, the sisters and brother had stood together as a family, these children who would be called upon to make desperate decisions on behalf of one another.

Shutter open, the photographer counted down the seconds … *twenty … nineteen … eighteen …* and came out from under his black cloth.

The family broke into separate people starting out on their walk home.

Minna is the eldest, the responsible child. She will become my goddess of wisdom and cookies, the one who will tell me family stories that I always believed, and who one day will choose to face the wrongs she has done.

Jen is the family daredevil, overlooked by her mother, defiant to her father, the one who will climb out a window to go dancing. "Do you love me?" she will ask me, and I won't answer just because she asked.

Bennie is the brother the sisters adored. He will teach them to play kick the ball, and at his Bar Mitzvah he will earn the rabbi's commendation, in hindsight an unwitting mockery: "This young man has a mind that will show itself in the future."

Helen is so small that only her head and a bit of her jersey are visible. Looking at this child, I can't believe I was once inside her. My mother will say to me, not once but many times, "I was a little nothing."

Pauline is her father's favorite, the infanta of the family gazing out from the sweet spot of his arm. She will grow up to tell me, "I was always the odd one out and so was my father, so we understood each other."

This is an absence for Francie, the youngest child, born too late to be included in the photograph.

AS MINNA WALKED home, she worried they'd find relatives who'd stayed on too long, beyond their mother's order: "Come only when my husband is out of the house." Entering the apartment and hearing the voices of lingerers—evidence of scheming behind his back—my grandfather fumed, packed a small bag, and took a streetcar to his tailor shop in Charlestown, where he slept on a cot, waking to brood about his superior but unrecognized intelligence.

My grandmother sent her children to plead with him to come back. They stood on the sidewalk, Minna next to Jen and then Helen, the three of them peering into the window like Little Match Girls, their father inside, his mustache bristling with familiar rage and unfamiliar power. He ignored them, going on cutting cloth until he could hold out no longer against their vigil.

Briefly a family again, they took the streetcar back to the apartment in Roxbury, where the parents went on flying at each other's throats. The girls made a circle to shut out the perverse actions of their mother, who, on getting what she wanted—her husband back—served him food she knew he hated. They watched as their father threw spinach and stewed blueberries against the wall, green slimy stuff sliding to the floor, blue juice dribbling down, leaving stains behind.

The circle was to last for the rest of their lives, women for whom the past was not a friend, to be countered by holding fast to that first linking of hands.

MY GRANDMOTHER WAS a person of emotions unmediated by deliberation. For my grandfather, emotions were for one thing only, rage. In all else he yearned for the cool life of the mind. On Sundays, he'd go to the Ford Hall Forum to listen to free lectures but come home frustrated because his English wasn't good enough to understand the speakers. Sometimes he'd take Minna or Jen to explain what the speakers were saying. When the girls were in their late teens, they may have heard Elizabeth Gurley Flynn giving a talk on "Labor and the Courts" or Charlotte Perkins Gilman on "What Feminism Is and Isn't." I never heard them speak of the substance, only of their pride at being able to translate the world for their father. But something outside the family, unconnected to Bennie's growing insanity, had to have entered into their young lives to turn them into the young women they became.

My grandparents' marriage was held together, Minna told me, by sexual attraction; in every other way they were toxic for each other, their tooth-and-claw battles played out on a field of mutual incomprehension. In the stories I've heard, they went on contending with each other in an almost routine way until Bennie was fourteen and began to change from a bright-eyed boy to a stranger who dropped a neighbor's cat from a roof, who stood frozen then ranted, spewing out words that made no sense. Because my grandfather refused to believe anything was wrong with his only son, my grandmother turned to her successful brother with worldly friends, among them a neurologist whom he asked to go to his poor sister in Roxbury and find out what was wrong with that boy of hers.

At his friend's behest, Abraham Myerson went to the chaotic apartment in Roxbury, examined Bennie, and delivered his diagnosis: Bennie was suffering from dementia praecox, meaning "adolescent-onset dementia" and known today as schizophrenia.

Sometimes diagnosis can be a relief, confirming that, yes, something is wrong and it has a name. Not so for my grandfather. Myerson's words struck him as a bolt thrown by a higher being, punishment for the curse he'd hurled at his wife when she'd been pregnant with Bennie.

"May there be a stone growing in your belly," he'd said.

"Myerson," which is what my family always called him, in verbal quotes, went on. "Your son hears voices nobody else can hear. They tell him that people—even you—are dangerous to him, so he has to hurt them. We don't know how to help people with Bennie's sickness. He'll have to spend the rest of his life in an asylum."

My grandfather, who had wanted to be the family god but never got beyond wrath, kicked the doctor out of the house. Then he turned back to Bennie—his son, his stone—and hurled his curse against the world.

BY THE TIME Myerson told my grandparents about Bennie's illness, he was already a notable figure, having served as one of the examining psychiatrists for the Sacco and Vanzetti trial and coming to believe in the anarchists' innocence. His expert prognosis about Bennie proved right. Soon after Myerson's visit, Bennie threatened his younger sisters with a kitchen knife. Minna quickly shepherded them out of the apartment and slid the bolt, knowing it had to be done but feeling bad at having to close the door against her brother.

When he came at them another time, it was clear: Bennie had to be committed to a nearby state hospital. That was the beginning of their mother's life of howling. She took one look at her son—a teenager locked in a filthy cell with madmen, syphilitics, and shell-shocked veterans—and threw herself on the floor, howling like a wolf in a Russian novel, stopping long enough to gather her forces and begin again: howl, pause, howl, pause, days of it until it was clear she'd go on howling until the hospital agreed to let Bennie out. When she brought Minna along one day to sign Bennie's release papers, the besieged hospital staff allowed him to go home, where he muttered, simmered, then erupted and attacked with whatever would serve as a weapon. Each time he had to be taken back to the asylum, where my grandmother would resume her howling and the same terrifying cycle would happen again and again.

Maybe it's because I don't have children, but it's hard for me to understand my grandmother's ferocity, focused single-mindedly on her son. Once Bennie became ill, there was no one to commiserate with her daughters, no one to wrap a bandage around a scraped knee, no one to say, "Don't cry, it's just a boo-boo." I've read about the excruciating pain a mother can feel for her wounded child. Can such a bond be denied? Not according to the mothers I've read about, the ones quoted in *Far From the Tree*, Andrew Solomon's book about parental caregiving: "I can't help myself," they say. But now, a world and time away from my grandmother, there are ways to help, things to do, pills to take, even though they often don't work. Then there was only the asylum, my grandmother's howl, the illusion of calm, the fact of mayhem. It is here that I come up against the dilemmas that run through this story. Self and other. Biology and conditions. Then and now. But first I have to face up to an uncomfortable truth, independent of all of the above: I never liked my grandmother. She wheedled to get her own way. And she should not have brought up her daughters—my own mother and aunts—to say, as Minna said to me, "We were so scared all the time."

Grandma and Bennie

IN 1926, MY grandfather left once and for all, packing his bag with no more in it than on previous departures, but with a stony silence that made it clear he'd no longer be responsive to entreaties to return. I can see how he could have persuaded himself that he had every right to leave, enough was enough, enough stewed blueberries, enough failure, enough howling. But his daughters heard a different message, one they took deep inside themselves: it was they who'd failed, who hadn't been able to make their father stay. Each felt abandoned, each in her own way.

When Minna was in her early twenties, she met the love of her life. "Leon liked to read," she said, "and you know me, I always had my head stuck in a book. He was gentle, kind. My sisters looked up to him, Pauline a little too much. She wanted to be his special little girl. You know Pauline—to this day I think she's jealous of me because of Leon.

"We'd go walking down Seaver Street," Minna continued—this was a story she told me many times—"and talk about where we were going to live when we got married, somewhere in Roxbury but away from our families, in our own house filled with books.

"One day Leon came over. He had a funny look. He said there was something he had to tell me.

"He hesitated but I was patient. I wanted to hear anything he had to say.

"He said his mother didn't want him to marry me. She was worried that Bennie's insanity would be passed on to her son's children.

"I waited to hear what Leon said back to her."

Minna paused, that moment clearer and more piercing than her present one.

"He said that he couldn't go against her wishes. I asked him what about me, what about all of us? We love you.

"I'll never forget his eyes filling with tears when he told me he'd miss us too."

Minna paused again, remembering that she felt a pain like

a knife stab. She ran to her room, where she kept the door shut for days.

"I heard my mother and sisters outside. They didn't know what to do and wondered whether they should take me to a hospital. I hated all of them. I hated Bennie. I hated myself. We weren't good enough for Leon."

Not good enough: my family's disease, an infection passed on by the first generation to the second, and then unavoidably caught by the next.

EVER DUTIFUL, MINNA married a hard-working, responsible man who had what it took to head up a fatherless household. Sam had grown up not with books as Leon had but with horses, holding their legs steady for his blacksmith father to shoe their hooves. At first Minna didn't consider Sam a possible suitor, but he wooed her, waiting at the door at the end of her workday as she covered her Underwood typewriter, walking her home so that she'd be safe, attentions not entirely unpleasant to a young girl still mourning her first love but in need of someone who cared for her.

For Helen, the younger sister who would become my mother, desire was in the air, evident in a snapshot of her at Nantasket Beach stretched out on the sand, one leg crossed over the other, smiling lazily into the camera. She must already have met the man who would become my father when he was driving an ice cream truck along Nantasket's dunes, a little tune announcing his arrival. Handing out popsicles, making change, he waited for my mother to show up so that he could give her the orange Creamsicle he'd saved especially for her. Little more than a boy, neglected by his parents, it must have been sunshine for him to see a smile on my mother's face.

My mother was transformed. "It was sex, pure sex," Minna once said to me. "I could walk right by them," she went on, "and they wouldn't even see me, they were so wrapped up in each other." Her tone was slightly aggrieved, as though in their erotic haze my parents had become defectors from the family. What's wrong with that, I wanted to ask but didn't because I knew the answer: I am part of it, a family so intertwined that to turn one's attention elsewhere was tantamount to betrayal. Besides, Minna was always skittish on the subject of sex. For her, the body was an afterthought once it had served its biological purposes. She told me sex had never been important to her, whereas my mother was always forthright about her physical love for my father. She'd bend down to kiss the top of his bald head and inhale, saying "I love the way you smell."

Sam and my father let in fresh air. They horsed around—I know this from a snapshot, the two of them in bathing suits, Sam sitting on my father's knee making a mock-horror face, my father grinning like a kid at a circus, tickled at having the clown on his lap. They kidded, cheerfully insulting each other, grilling hot dogs on weekends, and working hard the rest of the time, priding themselves on their strength. My father said of himself, "I'm an ox." Neither man was put off by the specter of Bennie; heredity didn't figure in their thoughts, and even if it had these men of strength with a root sense of inadequacy would have thought it was something to be overcome by their love and their need.

HEREDITY WAS ON people's minds. A newspaper article that perhaps Leon's mother had read reported on the 1925 Eastern States Exposition in Springfield, Massachusetts: "Among the booths on the Avenue of the States was an especially popular one that gave out prizes not for the best livestock but for the best human stock." Every fifteen seconds a red light blinked to show that another one hundred dollars of people's taxes had been spent to take care of a person with bad heredity. If defective people were a drain on society, as the eugenicists argued, then there was no reason for them to propagate.

Abraham Myerson, who publicly condemned forced sterilization, wrote, "I still remember the chaos that burst into my purposes and ideals when ... a biologist whom I greatly respected said that ... by keeping alive the unfit, we doctors were allowing those who would naturally die early to survive and pollute the race with their weakness and pathology ... helping the underdog was therefore racially destructive."

The shadow of eugenics supported the not-good-enough disease, not only my family's but the one that infects all the people who feel they can never measure up. Abraham Myerson wrote, "I was part of a group that studied certain great American families, families whose names are incorporated in the very warp and woof of American achievement and form part of the legend and tradition of American life. As we delved into hospital records and unearthed the bald statements incorporated in probate courts, we found among these families mental disease galore, yet the genealogies of these great American families made no mention of those members who had been incarcerated in hospitals for mental disease or judged insane by a court. So far as the family tree was concerned, every apple that hung from it was luscious and red. The complete records told a story of considerable decayed and distorted fruit."

That perfect tree helped with the image these families wanted to protect. To the sick—hidden away, erased—it was an image of shame. Those apples, desirable as perfect pearls, were evidence that they, the flawed and misshaped, were expendable.

This is a story that never ends; the eugenicists' platform resonates in today's debates about social welfare and so-called entitlements. It pointed the way toward lobotomy; if some people were considered not good enough to exist, there was no reason not to experiment on them. In 1933, a Disney animated short, *The Mad Doctor*, put Mickey Mouse and his faithful dog Pluto into the clutches of an evil brain surgeon who was experimenting with crossbreeding. Some sixty years later, in the 1995 animated film *Runaway Brain*, Mickey has a similar encounter when he knocks on a door and is sucked down into a laboratory where his brain is switched with that of an insane monster. A sign pointed Mickey's way; the doctor lives on a street called Lobotomy Lane.

IN 1935, EMINENT scientists from around the world converged in London for the Second International Neurological Congress, an event that would one day spiral down to a small point: an apartment in Roxbury.

John Fulton, Sterling Professor of Medicine at Yale, traveled to the Congress on the Normandie, the new ocean liner that was the latest word in luxury, its first-class dining room longer than the Hall of Mirrors at Versailles. Packed away with his J. Cross ties and his favorite 1848 Madeira was the paper Fulton was to deliver on two chimpanzees, Becky and Lucy. Back in his New Haven primate laboratory, the chimps had been violent, mean, fouling their cages when they didn't get what they wanted. But when Fulton and his colleagues surgically removed their frontal lobes for an experiment unrelated to the chimps' moods, they were astonished to see that Becky and Lucy came out of the operation, in the words of Fulton's associate, "as though they had joined a happiness cult." They were calm, docile, and spookily compliant.

Another neurologist, Egas Moniz, took the train from his native Lisbon; awaiting him at the Congress was a display that covered the entire exhibition hall of the Congress, a celebration of his discovery of cerebral angiography, a technique that yielded images of how blood flows through the brain. Debonair and cultivated in the Iberian tradition of the citizen-diplomat, he had represented his country at the signing of the Treaty of Versailles.

At a special session on the frontal lobes, a young American pathologist, Walter Freeman, sat next to Moniz. Freeman was attending the events on the coattails of his grandfather, William Williams Keen, America's first brain surgeon; at the Congress Walter was called—not always fondly—"the grandson." Already he was known for disdaining routine work; as a student he had poured urine samples down the drain so that he could concentrate on more interesting tasks of his own devising.

When the medical men listened to Fulton's presentation, the frontal lobes were relatively unknown territory; Phineas Gage, the railroad man of iconic fame from the iron rod that blasted through his skull destroying a frontal lobe, remained a nineteenth-century cluster of symptoms. As his friends said, "Gage was no longer Gage," but why this personality change had occurred wasn't yet known. Becky and Lucy's reactions to their surgeries suggested that moods could be altered but not why.

After Fulton's presentation, Moniz stood up to ask (and this is supposedly his exact language, as reported years later by Fulton): "If removal of the frontal lobes eliminates experimental neurosis in animals, would it not be possible to bring relief to human beings through such surgical means?" It's a good story, screenworthy in the tradition of thirties biographical films: Paul Muni as Emile Zola rising from his seat to argue on behalf of Alfred Dreyfus. With his black toupee perfectly parted down the center, his air of being equally at home at elegant dinner parties as with patients, Moniz was well positioned to gain the attention of the assembled scientists who themselves may have had similar as yet unexpressed thoughts. It is odd then that there is no record of this question in the notes of the Congress; everything else was meticulously documented. It may have been, however, only Fulton's latter-day attempt to impose a narrative, or perhaps to assign blame.

But in the year the Congress took place blame was far from anyone's mind. London was celebrating George V's Silver Jubilee, setting out to show its guests a good time while ignoring the stirrings of fascism. Moniz's Portugal was already under the right-wing rule of Antonio Salazar; the Spanish Republic was about to fall to Franco; a report by the Gestapo issued a few months before the Congress stated that the Nazi Party would be setting in motion a solution to the "Jewish problem." A month and a half after the Congress, Germany would put into effect the Nuremberg Race Laws.

Scientists and spouses danced to the tune of the musical then playing at London's Palace Theater, *Anything Goes*:

> *The world has gone mad today*
> *And good's bad today*
> *And black's white today*
> *And day's night today*

It is tempting to see Cole Porter's song as background music to the story of lobotomy. But to do so would require the proverbial eyes in the back of one's head. For the participants, especially those who traveled to the Congress and sat in on that fateful session, no such perspective troubled them. Instead a grand vista lay ahead—anticipation for a glorious future in which these men had every hope and expectation of making their mark.

3.

IN 1940, ABRAHAM MYERSON KNOCKED AT OUR FAMILY'S door once again. In the years since he had diagnosed Bennie, his reputation had soared. He held prestigious posts, among them professor of clinical psychiatry at Harvard University. He was director of his own research laboratory, had authored several influential books and chaired the American Neurological Association's Commission on Eugenics. He achieved even greater prominence when *Time* magazine hailed his discovery of the first antidepressant, a new drug that gave patients renewed energy and motivation. His entrance heralded stupendous news: at last, something could be done for Bennie.

Word of lobotomy had reached American shores. After the Congress, Egas Moniz had headed back to Portugal, where he devised an instrument for entering the brain; he called it a leuco-tome from the Greek word for white, referencing the white matter that was to be cut, the connective tissue that was to be interrupted. It was soon nicknamed the apple corer because it looked so much like that household implement. Moniz selected eleven female patients from the Lisbon insane asylum for the experimental operation. There was no such thing then as informed consent; the postwar code that set out guidelines for ethical human experimentation would not come along for another eleven years, but even if regulations had been in place, I doubt they'd have made a difference. Limits were conveniently overlooked before and have been since. For several weeks following the operations, Moniz observed the changes in his patients, becoming more and more jubilant as the women became as docile and undisturbed as Becky and Lucy. Eager to plant his flag on this new territory, Moniz quickly wrote a monograph proclaiming his procedure a success and rushed to the post office to get it out on the last train that night.

It landed on the desk of Walter Freeman, who had been asked to review it. Sitting in his office at Washington DC's St. Elizabeth's Hospital, the doctor in Freeman was excited: at last, a way to help the mentally ill; even as the snubbed grandson in Freeman saw the way to make a reputation that would be his and his alone. Even before the first lobotomy was performed in the United States, Freeman began to promote this new operation, waylaying reporters, talking up its wonders, giving them scoops. In turn they wrote articles with headlines like: "Psychosurgery Cured Me"; the crazily wrong-headed, "No Worse Than Removing A Tooth"; and my own favorite, evocative of those Disney animations, "Wizardry Of Surgery Restores Sanity To Fifty Raving Maniacs."

Imagine Myerson, pedagogical to the core, sitting in Minna's living room, explaining the new operation to my aunts: "There are two prefrontal lobes deep behind the eyebrows where other parts of the brain send signals, like the ones from Bennie's emotional centers that tell him a person is dangerous. The signals travel through the white matter; when they reach the lobes, they turn into a plan of action and Bennie attacks. Think of the white matter as a switchboard. We will interrupt it so that one part of Bennie's brain can't send messages to the other. I promise you: nothing will be removed—only disconnected."

Disconnected. Damnedest thing about lobotomy. Even though the operation is viewed with horror, it was also a creative leap into the understanding of mental illness, surmising that it was a problem with communication between areas of the brain. Lobotomy itself, however, was a premature and crude application of a brilliant insight that had become corrupted by the pursuit of personal glory. Several months after Moniz sent out his monograph, many of his patients relapsed, as did John Fulton's Lucy, the unfortunate chimpanzee who went back to being as hostile and destructive as before. The world heard nothing about these reversals and none of the already-published findings were modified.

IN THEIR TWENTIES and mid-thirties, my mother and aunts were caught in something they couldn't fully comprehend, invented by men far away from them in geography and status, hampered in their decision by believing they weren't good enough. They brought to the decision all the tangled strands of their lives—the fear that had begun in their childhoods and had never left them, their awe of people they saw as "higher," their sense of responsibility, and their yearning for something they'd never known—a normal life, or at least their image of it. "Normal" would come to mean post-war conformity; when I heard the word as I was growing up, I thought it was a death sentence. By 1960 the teenaged character in the new musical *The Fantasticks* said, "Please God, please, don't let me be normal!" Now though I feel its pathos. "You can't imagine what it was like," Minna once said, "with all the conflict going on all the time. It was a madhouse. We never had anyone around who was normal."

And in all of it they were alone. The husbands worked all the time. My grandfather was gone.

My grandmother had to have weighed in on the fate of her son but I've never heard her mentioned as having any part in the decision; I think by this time her obsession with Bennie had made her unable to weigh pros and cons. All she wanted was whatever would keep her son safe and at home with her. It was up to the sisters.

When my mother and aunts sat down in Minna's living room to discuss their brother's fate, Minna, always the reader, might have cited an article that appeared on the front page of a 1939 issue of the New York Times: "There must be at least 200 men and women in the United States who have had worries, persecution complexes, suicidal intentions, obsessions, indecisiveness, nervous tension, cut out of their minds …"

"They say it works," Minna said. "But will it be good for Bennie?"

"Myerson says so. But what if it doesn't work?" Helen, my mother, replied.

"Look, what if we do it?" Jen asked, restless, always in favor of the unknown. "Suffering isn't doing him any good."

Helen said, "But it will take money—they say he'll need a caretaker."

Jen had begun to realize that her talent lay in making money. "I can help with that," she assured her sisters.

Did they understand that ridding Bennie of his unbearable feelings would mean that he'd be left with no feelings at all? Could anyone comprehend such a condition, such a life?

"Is there anyone else we can talk to?" Minna asked.

It was then that the sisters took on the family roles that would characterize them for the rest of their lives, traits that I grew up thinking were their natures but now understand were also formed and deformed by their lives: Minna unsure but wanting everyone to pull in the same direction; Jen leaning toward action without a safety net; Helen combining diffidence with practicality.

Minna added, "What do you think will happen if we don't do it?"

"What do you think?" Jen answered in her no-nonsense way. "He'll keep hurting people."

Minna took offense at the implied rebuke: hadn't she learned anything after what Bennie did to Dan?

WHEN MINNA GAVE birth to little Dan, the first child in the family, all the sisters were at the ready to watch over his cradle, keeping him under their eyes like loving hawks. But the circle of protection didn't hold. In the midst of a longish lull in Bennie's madness, Minna told herself it was all right to drop off four-year old Dan at her mother's apartment, just for a few minutes while she ran a quick errand. But Minna hadn't counted on how fast Bennie's good spells could turn bad. Alone in the living room with his little nephew, Bennie hit him. He kept on trying to hurt him. Dan scrambled behind a chair, where he was still crouched when Minna came home. She picked up her son and held him against her thin chest while he burrowed his head under her arm. She was anguished for her suffering child and frightened too about what Sam might do when he came home later.

Bennie's blows must have gone on landing in Dan's mind. Years later, when Dan was a grown man, I could hear the bitterness in his voice when he said that this—not a goodnight kiss, not a rubber duckie—was his first memory.

"What was my mother doing," Dan asked angrily years later, "leaving me with that madman?"

It's a good question. Minna had been trying to make that normal life for her family, and that life included her love for Bennie, the brother he had been and the suffering creature he'd become. Now she was horrified. She blamed herself for what had happened; she'd already known there was a demon inside him. What kind of a person was she, to put her child in danger?

Brother and son. It's almost Biblical. Which do you choose to sacrifice?

PAULINE, THEN IN her early twenties, wasn't present for the discussion and its aftermath. She had married George, the first white-collar worker in the family, a chemical engineer who'd brought her to Delaware, where he became an expert on dyes. Pauline and George were starting out on a life that would be lived apart from her sisters.

FRANCIE, THE YOUNGEST sister, also wasn't part of the decision; she was too young, born out of the last remnant of her parents' sexual passion before their marriage imploded. Francie watched silently as her older sisters left the family house—Minna, Helen, and Pauline going forth to marriage, Jen to business—until she was the last sister left in the family apartment, alone with her mother and Bennie. Francie had never known Bennie as the lovely brother Pauline remembered; she was three years old when he was diagnosed with schizophrenia and knew him only as someone to be feared.

Francie had always been timid and withdrawn, but she was becoming more so. Had Bennie attacked her, as he had little Dan only a short while ago? Her other sisters agreed: she shouldn't stay in the apartment. One day, Minna went to her mother, explained what had to happen and gathered up Francie's things. I picture the oldest and the youngest of the sisters walking the few blocks to Minna and Sam's apartment, Francie carrying a bag with her belongings, Minna holding her other hand.

"She was like my child," Minna said. "I'd ask her do you need anything and she'd always say yes."

Francie was fourteen when she made the move. Dan, much younger, remembers her as "always wonderful to me. She was more like an older sister than an aunt. She only wanted everything to be good for me."

He also remembers that Francie could change in an instant into "the neediest person I've ever met. If someone didn't smile at her, she'd cry. It wasn't a matter of patching up a bad day, that was how she was."

THE FINAL DECISION to go ahead with Bennie's lobotomy must, I think, have been based on faith in Myerson who was, after all, familiar—a Russian Jew from the same wave of immigration as their mother's—and also a higher mortal endowed with authority. The older sisters lived in a world where they believed there were exalted people like Myerson and little people like themselves.

Like so many in my generation who came of age in the sixties, I grew up impatient with the idea of submission to any supposedly higher authority. When the Internet came along, I chose to place my faith in information. When a problem arises, my first recourse is to seek out a solution by asking questions of a search engine. I start out believing that if I'm sufficiently resourceful, answers can and will be found.

As I get older though, I have a growing suspicion that my devotion to information has been misplaced. It's not so much that I don't believe in searching—it's that I no longer believe in the usefulness of answers. I've seen that there are problems that can't be solved no matter how many "answers" one finds. Illness brings this home—we learn and learn about what's wrong and still we suffer. Information ends with an often inadequate answer; knowledge goes on questioning.

HERE IS WHAT was done to Bennie: holes were drilled in his skull; the blade of an instrument was inserted through the holes, its handle swung as far and deep as possible.

This description is as brief as I can mercifully make it.

Merciful be damned. I have no reason to spare anyone. I am writing a story that I haven't faced for many years. I can't let myself avoid it now, even though I myself have been made so squeamish that I had to put down Eliot Valenstein's groundbreaking 1986 book on lobotomy, *Great and Desperate Cures*, when I read "the instrument was withdrawn, [and] pieces of healthy brain tissue came out with it."

So much for Myerson's claim that nothing would be removed. Because the surgeons had no way to see inside the skull, their wild cuts permanently damaged the lobes.

I steeled myself and picked up the book again. "Having observed," Valenstein writes, "that the optimum results were achieved when the lobotomy induced drowsiness and disorientation … the surgeons asked patients to sing a song, or to perform arithmetic, and if they see no signs of disorientation, they cut away more." It is reliably reported that when Rosemary Kennedy, the sister of President John F. Kennedy, was lobotomized by Walter Freeman she was asked to sing "God Bless America." Like all the others, 5,000 by 1941, Bennie must have added and subtracted, multiplied and divided, sung "Mary Had a Little Lamb" all the way to oblivion. *Little lamb, little lamb … its fleece was white as snow …*

AS HE HAD SO many times before, Bennie was brought home from the hospital. He looked more or less the same. But he was not as he had been. He didn't speak. He walked slowly, and once he sat down he barely moved. He didn't react to anything or anyone around him.

His sisters waited for him to emerge from what seemed like a prolonged unnatural half-sleep, frightened he'd take up his old violent ways. Then—perhaps suddenly, perhaps gradually—they realized that this was the way Bennie was going to be. Minna, who only wanted to think nice thoughts, once said something to me that must have shocked her with its implicit admission of relief at what their brother had become.

She said, "We weren't scared anymore."

4.

Bennie after his lobotomy

THIS IS BENNIE AS I KNEW HIM MANY YEARS LATER. When I'd visit him with my mother, he'd open the door of the apartment, his eyes dull, unchanging when he saw us standing in the doorway, a little girl and her mother seeking entrance. He'd acknowledge us with a small upturning of lips—not a smile, more of a grimace—then with his eyes averted, he'd lean forward and for an instant graze his stubbly cheek against mine. He reached out his hand and touched me behind my ear. To this day, I can still feel his touch. No one can touch me there. I flinch.

Bennie would silently turn back to the living room, where he sat in his overstuffed armchair, crocheted doilies on the arms to protect it from his sweat. He held a magazine in his lap, turning its pages without looking down. My mother and I would head off in the other direction, down the hallway to the kitchen, where my grandmother held court amid her collection of the ordinary crazy people—the ones who hadn't been labeled as such but who included her brother, who spent his days in that kitchen wearing an undershirt and suspenders, arguing with the newspaper, punching a finger into its pages to make his point.

Those were years when my mother and aunts flourished, their lives no longer filled with menace. They settled into the rhythm of everyday life, of individual pleasures and family solidarity, of day-to-day problems that could be managed.

Helen, Francie, Jen, Pauline, Minna

I GREW UP surrounded by these women, this mother, these aunts, by their soft skin, pale pink nail polish, powder, beige nylons in a drawer, china pitchers for milk—never cartons!—women who were stylish, aware of how they looked, how they presented themselves to the world.

When I was young, my aunts carried a kind of glamour, a sense of autonomy: an aunt could come and go bearing delight as Pauline did—a cake with ribbons hanging from it, and when I pulled at one, out would come something wonderful at its end, a little horse, a ring.

Sometimes I felt an aunt, singly, to be my ally, not in an argument—we didn't do much of that—but in empathy. At other times, they were "the sisters," a single impregnable unit.

Often, though, I could feel an undercurrent of worry: Was I okay? Would I be all right?

One of their most important roles for me was to confer double vision. At first, I saw them only through my mother's eyes. With no brothers or sisters, I didn't have any measure of comparison, no shared stockpile of memories. But my aunts showed me that people could take on different facets. Their presence allowed me to observe, to take up my own point of view.

FOR A WHILE longer, the sisters stayed on in Roxbury living in three-decker apartments, as I did later—a clapboard three-story building, one apartment on top of another, their layouts exactly the same. Three-decker lives were lived in stacks and extended back several generations. I have a photograph of my mother as a child sitting with a friend on the front steps of the building where she grew up. I could place another photo over it, me with another little girl, and the two images would line up like the apartments themselves.

Bennie lived a three-decker life. He was never left alone, never abandoned to his own vast incapacities. His sisters rallied around him, surrounded him, provided for him. I have a friend who finds this amazing; to my family it was second nature. On the basis of a follow-up study, Walter Freeman concluded that Jews who had undergone lobotomies had the best outcomes because strong family ties kept them safe at home. We were living proof.

From the beginning, Jen paid for all of Bennie's and her mother's needs. A caretaker lived in the apartment, bathing and dressing Bennie, taking him on long, mute walks. Mr. Adams stayed on for years, a narrow-faced man who always seemed to be wearing a suit and tie. When he took Bennie out, he wore a felt hat with a center crease and a hatband, an ensemble so formal and specific that I can see him to this day.

Jen had started out working at a department store in Cambridge's Central Square, a ratty place where she caught the eye of Moe, the buyer. He noticed that she was shrewd, with an instinct for knowing what styles customers wanted. He took his savings and backed her to open her own competing clothing store around the corner. Jen named it The Emily Rose Shoppe, Neither Emily nor Rose was a name known in our family; Jen always said she'd chosen them because they sounded gentle to her, which has always seemed sad to me knowing that gentleness was not something she had experienced growing up and, like so much else, something Jen had to provide for herself.

She didn't need those notes of gentility, the double "pp" and that last "e": the women who were her customers—beauticians, office workers, saleswomen—liked it that Jen was one of their own, a worker too. Although soon she was earning enough money to hire help, she always insisted on being the one to go down to the basement and haul up new shipments of clothes hanging from heavy metal racks. Her sisters saw her as a martyr to the store, exploited by Moe and her own masochism. Then again, they were never responsible for the success of a business, not to mention one that would soon have a loyal clientele.

When Moe got fired—his boss found out he'd set Jen up in a rival business—he walked over to The Emily Rose Shoppe and told Jen what had happened.

"Well, get to work," she said.

Jen and Moe made a go of it in business and in bed. Jen had had boyfriends before Moe—Frankie the ballroom dancer (not Jewish!) and Gerry, who just didn't have enough oomph. None of them had Moe's drive. He was the right partner for Jen, but he was already married and living pleasantly in suburban Newton with every intention of staying there.

From time to time Jen got away from the store on weekends, talked into it by Moe. They'd go to Cuba, America's safety valve in the forties, a place where people could lose their inhibitions knowing they'd find them again on their return. Sometimes Moe had to cancel a trip at the last minute. He didn't explain—it was obvious, his family had to come first. He suggested that Jen take her youngest sister Francie in his place: "Give her a good time, get her out of her shell."

FRANCIE HAD GOT a job as a filing clerk at a downtown company where the family had connections. The night before she started work, she was so nervous that Minna sat up for hours trying to reassure her.

"Francie," Minna said, "you know we all love you, we never think badly of you when you take things hard, that's the way you're made, but that doesn't mean you have to give up, you can do it."

At the end of her first day on the job, Francie walked into Minna's house, all the way back down the linoleum hallway to the kitchen, into a corner where she stood silently facing the wall.

"What's the matter?" Minna asked.

Francie's shoulders heaved.

"Tell me, what's wrong," Minna said. "Did anything bad happen?"

Francie wept, "I can't do it." That was all she would say. "I can't. I can't."

Minna didn't mention that the family needed the money Francie brought in. But Francie must have guessed because she went back to work, fighting her fears so that she could do what had to be done for the family.

JEN TOOK MOE up on his suggestion and brought Francie along with her to Cuba, to the legendary Havana of gangsters and showgirls. They stayed at the glamorous Hotel Nacional, with its sweeping palm-lined driveway, its loggia in the back where guests sat in rattan chairs looking out at the Gulf of Mexico as waiters served them cocktails.

At night in the dining room, there were floorshows featuring bandleaders like Bebo Valdes and his orchestra shaking maracas in their blindingly white ruffled shirts. Openhanded with tips, Jen was always given her favorite table close to the stage. Men in white dinner jackets, good looking but too smooth, gave her the once-over; a type that always moved in on her but were met with rebuff, at least when she was with her kid sister. Instead of flirting back, Jen turned away and tapped out a cigarette from her gold mesh case. She'd go through a pack a night, each held in the position that signaled sophistication, elbow on table, forearm straight and turned outward, palm bent back from the wrist, the cigarette held almost horizontally. Sometimes the smoke gave her a dry little cough.

YEARS LATER, WHEN I visited Castro's Cuba, I stayed in that same hotel, still with its sweeping driveway and loggia, now inhabited by the ghosts of my aunts, such powerful presences to me still. I saw them there as they'd been in photographs, Jen in ankle strap shoes, Francie in a shortsleeved blouse, sitting side-by-side in those rattan chairs, dark glasses concealing what they might have been feeling.

Jen had to be angry with Moe for canceling the trip. But it wouldn't do to let down her discipline. She'd taken over this trip by herself, carried it off with panache. She could do what she wanted in a man's world—everything but make someone choose her and only her to love. She needed that love so badly that one day she'd seize it, taking Francie with her.

5.

December 7, 1941

"IT IS WITH VARIED EMOTIONS THAT I WRITE THE EDITORIAL for the *Circle News* this month. As we all know, war with all its horror has suddenly come upon us."

Minna began to write a newsletter that she read aloud at family meetings, ranking the U.S.'s entrance into World War II ahead of Francie's news but not by much.

"The next important event of the month, as we are all aware, is, of course, Francie's beautiful watch, which Harry gave her the first day of Chanukah. Francie is cute—all smiles—not to say anything about J. Harold Gurstein. Let us hope that they will continue to be happy always."

Francie's happiness was big news to her sisters. Always a blusher, she must have turned rosy when Harry came courting in his diffident way. They'd been fixed up by relatives; soon Harry was installed in our living room, the newest husband, cutting a pack of cards for a game with my father.

Harry was peculiar. Something wasn't right: he was too white, too flabby and hairless.

"I doubt very much they ever had sex," my mother said when I asked her many years later, my father adding that Harry's testicles had never descended. With Harry, though, Francie's most important need was satisfied. He was her ally; now she would be safe.

On September 22, 1942, the *Circle News* reported a new development, written in the effusive good cheer that was not Minna's natural element but is, I think, evidence of her will to keep everyone together.

"First, of course, and of major importance is Harry's entrance into the army of our country. Are we proud of Harry! We all miss him very much, especially Francie. We don't blame her a bit as we all know that love is wonderful and we, too, miss his smiling face. However, we are proud and we know that it has to be thus, so good luck Harry, and our sincere hope that soon you will be back with all of us again."

IN 1942, WALTER Freeman and his colleague James Watts published their influential book, *Psychosurgery. Intelligence, Emotion and Social Behavior Following Prefrontal Lobotomy for Mental Disorders*. Freeman had drawn the design for the book's cover, deriving the image from the French expression for feeling depressed: *J'ai des papillons noirs*, or "I have black butterflies." Often depressed himself, Freeman drew a skull with a hole through which black butterflies flew to freedom. Freeman persuaded the publisher to ship copies of the first printing to England, but the boat that carried the books was sunk by a German submarine.

THE U.S. MILITARY had to have been hard up—Harry wasn't exactly soldier material. Settled into a desk job at the Reno Army Air Base, he was able to send for Francie. At first she didn't want to leave Boston and the family but she let herself be talked into it by Minna.

Harry took Francie horseback riding, a daring activity for two anxious Jews. As Francie rode up the trail behind Harry, her slow horse walking through the shadows of white pines, she wondered what her sisters would say if they could see her. On leave, Harry and Francie went to San Francisco. Neither had seen anything like the city of steep hills where it seemed everywhere they looked was bay or bridge. They splurged and stayed at Cliff House, where they watched the seals. I picture them walking through Chinatown, eating cautiously, peering into shops, buying a little gong. At a jazz club in the Fillmore District, they heard Count Basie. Sometimes she even forgot to wonder what her sisters would say.

I want to cheer her on—Go, Francie, go.

BUT HARRY BEGAN to disappear at night. Alone in the apartment on the army base, Francie tried to wait up for him but he'd come in too late, sometimes at two or three in the morning.

She phoned Minna.

"Don't worry, Francie," Minna reassured her. "You'll see, it will turn out to be nothing."

The phone calls became more urgent.

"I hate to say this, Francie, but do you think he could be cheating on you?" Minna asked with trepidation.

Francie got up her nerve and began to ask around a bit. It turned out that the husband of a friend had seen Harry at one of the casinos that lined Reno's Virginia Street strip. Harry's love affair, it turned out, was with gambling.

Minna said, "Maybe you should talk to him … ?"

One night Francie waited up until the early hours of the morning. When Harry came home, she confronted him.

He lashed out. "Mind your own business. I'm doing what I feel like doing for a change."

When Minna heard about Harry's being so mean she couldn't believe this was the same man who had read comic books in her living room.

My mother could. "We've always known he's weak. He hates himself because he can't stand up to temptation, so he takes it out on her."

Francie wept so much that Harry didn't know what to do for her. A doctor gave her a prescription for a sedative, which helped, and Harry began to be nicer to her. I think he wanted to be a good man and in his own way he loved her, enough to try to withstand his own demons for as long as he could.

His military service over, Harry drove the two of them across the country. He wanted to make a detour to see the Grand Canyon but Francie didn't want to stop. Nor did she want to see the Great Plains, its expanse so different from what she was looking forward to in Boston: a safe protected space.

MY MOTHER AND aunts were busy building a nest for Harry and Francie's return. They rented a small undemanding apartment in Allston, Jen paying for the furnishings and my mother doing the decorating.

"It was adorable, like a dollhouse," my mother said to me years later, recalling for me Pauline's dollhouse and making me shudder at her pleasure in making things fit within a small compass.

"I found a nice bedroom set and some pretty curtains at Gilchrist's. They were on sale so I got some extra material for a dust ruffle."

She bought them a maple headboard and footboard with carved finials topping the bedposts, and matching chest of drawers, each drawer with two round knobs.

Candlestick lamps, brass, with scalloped trim shades, one on each side of the bed.

Cornices above the windows, covered in the same fabric as the curtains and dust ruffle.

A dinette set made of Formica in the splatter pattern.

A set of Franciscan earthenware dishes for every day in the popular Desert Rose pattern, light yellowish bowls encircled with wide rims of raised pink roses and green vines, carrying a tinge of the Southwest, of a different life.

I have inherited those Desert Rose bowls. They remain eloquent. They speak of postwar coziness, of the glaze of security, the lull of false safeties.

AS MINNA AND Sam's son Dan grew to become an adolescent, Abraham Myerson noticed that he was a bright boy, curious about the wider world. Myerson, closer to our family after his own son had married a relative of ours, took Dan under his wing, his tutelage making Minna proud and Sam a little irritated at Dan's worship of a person whose breadth of experience was so far beyond his own. Neither seemed to question Myerson's wisdom in steering Bennie to his lobotomy; the world of heroes did not admit of questions.

Dan said of Myerson, "He was my university. We had wide-ranging talks, never about me. He was austere, intimidating to some people. Not to me—sometimes he'd call me on Sunday and ask me to bring over some 'Good Jewish rye bread—unsliced! Sliced bread is an abomination.'"

Dan remembers sitting opposite Myerson when he pushed a Rorschach test across his desk, asking Dan, "What does that look like to you?" Dan studied it and replied, "A fat lady with a dog on a leash."

Myerson asked with rhetorical ire, "So—do *you* see a penis?"

HIS SCOFFING WAS of a piece with beliefs he shared with other psychiatrists of his time. Convinced that mental illness originated in the body, they espoused bodily interventions, among them lobotomy. While medical historians have written narratives in which somaticists and Freudians are seen as stern opponents, in the thirties what was then called *mental medicine* encompassed many forms. As noted by Jack Pressman in *Last Resort: Psychosurgery and the Limits of Medicine,* at one conference, "the delegates included Adolf Meyer on psychobiology, Lawrence Kubie on psychoanalysis, A.L. Kroeber on anthropology and Abraham Myerson on physiological psychiatry ... Kubie expounded upon the Freudian revolution that was overturning every discipline's conception of human nature; at the same time neuropathologist Walter Freeman declared his faith that only chemical research would at last 'dissolve the mists that surround the one irresistible conclusion that faulty cortical function is synonymous with psychosis.'"

Lobotomy was spreading, in no small part due to Freeman and Watts's book—in 1945, there were 150 operations, while by 1947 the number rose to almost 2,000 and was soon to double. In hindsight, it seems evident that the operation was also a pawn in a war with the Freudians, whose sun by then was rising and threatening to eclipse the influence of the somaticists. These were not minor battles: turf, prizes, and privileges came along with the winner. Both sides were passionate about the health of their patients; dedication and fervor were mixed with grandiosity and glory.

But nothing is ever one-sided. Anti-Freudian as Myerson was, he helped to bring Freudian analysts from Nazi Germany to the United States, arranging for them to get green cards and licenses to practice because, in his words as quoted by his son, "they were good people." The story of lobotomy is the story of paradox.

SOON DAN WOULD need Myerson's friendship. One day, Minna asked my father to tighten a loose spring on the screen door. Later that day when Dan started out to the backyard, the door—now too tight—banged into him, its latch hitting one eye with such force that it ulcerated and he had to lose it. Afterward he developed a facial tic that looked as though he was trying to wink but never quite achieving it, and so trying again and again. Referring to himself in the third person in an essay he wrote in his fifteenth year, he asked, "Could he tell of his boyhood? Of that lonely, imaginative and wondering time in which he played at being everybody but himself? ... Could he tell of his accident and his illness, of that which altered the channels of his mind and of the burning complexes and inhibitions it had caused, of the nervous reaction that had followed and left a scar on his mind that was not yet healed?"

Dan already knew the answer.

No.

He couldn't risk telling, because even the hint that something might be wrong would make his mother worry that he might be getting sick like Bennie, and her worry would trespass on his inner life, bringing to it a background noise of anxious clucking. To tell was also to be vulnerable to intrusions: "What are you writing, Dan?" When I saw a production of Tennessee Williams's *The Glass Menagerie*, I was struck by a director's moment—Amanda, the mother, trying to look over her son's shoulder to see what he is writing, Tom throwing himself over his typewriter, hugging it to keep the page from her eyes.

Minna could see for herself that Dan was disturbed and asked Doctor Myerson for his advice. Although Myerson had been skeptical of Freud and what he thought were his unscientific methods, he took Dan to a psychiatrist who was the daughter of Viennese analyst Alfred Adler, part of Freud's inner circle until he was cast out for putting forward his theory of the inferiority complex—or what I might call in my family the not-good-enough complex. When his clinics were shut down by the Nazis, Adler and his daughter Alexandra left Vienna and emigrated to Boston, where

Alexandra Adler had a private practice in Kenmore Square. It was there that Myerson took Dan. She was a good choice; she was conducting what would turn out to be a pioneering study of what we now call post-traumatic stress. After Boston's Coconut Grove fire—the deadliest nightclub fire in history, killing almost five hundred people and injuring hundreds more—Adler undertook interviews with the survivors to learn the psychological and physical consequences of trauma. She herself knew firsthand what it had been like to escape from danger, to survive while behind her others burned. With Dan, she knew what it was like to struggle with the aftermath of one's own trauma.

SHE BEGAN EACH session by asking Dan what he had in his pockets. He got a kick out of that, but more vivid yet was the time he spent in her waiting room reading Anne Morrow Lindbergh's book *North to the Orient*. Dan had to have known about Charles Lindbergh's 1927 plane flight around the world and his wife's subsequent journeys as his co-pilot. He had to know too about the tragedy that befell the couple when their child was kidnapped and murdered.

Did Dan also know that Anne Morrow Lindbergh had publicly disclosed that she had suffered a serious depression, that writing *North to the Orient* had been her way to rescue herself? In a waiting room, carried away by a book, Dan began to get a glimpse of how writing could rescue him too.

Later I would come to feel the same way about writing, discovering that putting what I felt into words was a counterweight to the disturbing presence of Bennie. When I was about seven, my mother and I were walking past a fruit and vegetable store, its produce piled in big canvas bags set out on the sidewalk. My mother said how sweet young peas were straight from the pod. She picked out a pod and snapped it. Bright green peas lay there in a row, four of them, each a little different from the next. She held out the open pod to me and snapped another for herself. Mmmm. We agreed, so sweet.

That pod, that canoe of greenness in my mother's palm … I could feel something stirring in me. When we got back to the house, I asked for a pad of paper. When I finished writing, I walked over to my mother and offered her my poem.

"Where did you come from?" she asked.

This question, I've since learned, is one that many parents ask at some time or another, wonderingly, that this miracle could have come from them. But I heard it differently, as though I were being consigned to a distant unknowable place, star-like but beyond the family pale, a place about which I had mixed feelings. I didn't want to be consigned to that pale, but I didn't want to be banished from it either. An embrace can feel protective even as it stifles.

Minna, though, knew where I came from; it was she who told me that I had inherited the "Writing Gene," her phrase for a compulsion to set down words that had popped up through several generations of the family and now, she said, had shown up again in me.

Minna herself had wanted to write, something I realized when I found the back room in her apartment with its typewriter, an anthology of poetry with her name on the flyleaf, and a stack of paper that did not diminish between my visits. That room was where I discovered the music of Dylan Thomas and W. H. Auden before I understood what their words meant. Even more important was my discovery that Minna had an inner life, different from the person I knew in the everyday life of the family.

Looking back, I see her in the words of psychoanalyst Alice Miller, who asks, "One troubled child channels her pain into art; another vents his anguish in destructive acts. What makes the critical difference in the way each translates childhood suffering?" Miller's answer is the presence of a "helping witness—someone who acts … with kindness toward the child and who somehow, by looking into the child's eyes, shows the child another way to live and be." For me, Minna was that witness. She had named the Writing Gene and anointed me to be next in line.

Without denying Miller her important insight, I think she elevates the helping witness to a position above the child, when sometimes the best witness bends down to look into the child's eyes. Minna put herself on the same level by the simple act of giving me her own experience so that we saw ourselves in each other.

6.

IN 1947, DAN WENT AWAY TO COLLEGE, THE FIRST IN THE family to do so. Minna sent him cookies and a warm coat. He wrote back, "It has got to the point where no matter what happens, no matter how many people there are with me, I have a terrible feeling of despair and fear, I feel as if the whole world is tied around my heartstrings and is dragging me down. All you seem to care about is cookies. Yes, the coat is here. The cookies aren't."

Minna must have felt frightened—what did she know to do besides worry about a warm-enough coat and send Dan the cookies he used to love? She went to her mother's successful brother, the one who'd brought Abraham Myerson into their lives, and asked him to give Dan the benefit of his wisdom.

"Dear Dan," he wrote, "For some people it is easy to be 'hail, fellow, well met' with everyone. For more complex personalities who are sensitive, shy and retiring, contact with others becomes frequently a painful process. The pain is more intense because it is aggravated by an opposing pull. On the one hand there is the longing to form with and commune with other personalities, and on the other the fear of contact with them. It is only when we permit the repelling force to overcome the attractive pull that we count failures in living ... "

Reading this now, I admire the tempered analysis, the parsing of pulls and personalities. Reading it then, though, I would have rebelled against that god-like tone, useless at a time when I was feeling passion and despair. It certainly did nothing for Dan.

"I've lost any desire to fight. I can't take it anymore, I'm all done in. But this I know—that it can't go on like this much longer."

Minna went to Doctor Myerson and asked him to be in touch with Dan. He wrote letters based on what he called "a new philosophy based on readjustment and the nobility of struggle."

"Dear Dan: Whatever has happened in the past is gone and you can make it as dead as a doornail ... Develop a tolerant reaction to the foibles and commonplace reactions of the people you deal with even if you find them disgusting. Study them as material. If you can do it, become one with them ... Avoid the overaesthetic and over-refined people. If they are necessary for you, use them, but they are not built solidly enough for a world which is unaesthetic and unrefined ... Join a fraternity or a social group, taking an easy and tolerant attitude towards the ritual and absurdity, which, when you boil them down, are necessary to social cohesion ... Put up a brave front. Do not show your feelings. Act so that you will not betray weakness or discourage others. The acting will become natural after a while."

To me, Myerson's advice to Dan—"you can make it as dead as a doornail"—has an Emersonian ring in the latter's exhortation to "bring the past for judgment into the thousand-eyed present, and live ever in a new day." I disagree: to live in the present is a very fine thing, but does it follow that the past should be made to die? I know that Myerson is saying that the past for Dan was an albatross. Believing in the power of will, he assures Dan that he can chuck this weight off his chest. But here's the rub: the past is always leaking into the present and no amount of will can stop that process. It is consciousness itself.

Much as Dan might have wanted to scream in frustration at Myerson's advice, he pleaded with his parents instead:

> They are taking something I wrote for the newspaper and they have asked me to write a story for the literary magazine and Jim wants me to try out for a play they're doing. As far as that goes I could be all right. But you can't imagine how it is. I can't go on like this much longer. I am at the end. I have a dull feeling that I cannot stand. I

don't mean to worry you but I can't keep it in all the time. It's too strong for me. Please. Isn't there something you can do?

Please please do something, because I can't stand it anymore.

Please,

Love,

Dan

What made Dan think that his parents could help? Minna was baffled, unable to think of anything but what she'd already done: go to Abraham Myerson and write pale echoes.

> You make me sick with the things you write back. Fight! What is there to fight? Don't you realize that I'm all fought out, all done ... My head aches and my stomach hurts and I get dizzy and tired and I hear bells in my head and the light seems to be getting dimmer and then bright again, all the time.

That's a scary letter. The bells and the lights could have been migraines, but to Minna they might have sounded like the onset of schizophrenia. Several months later, the dean of the college wrote to my aunt and uncle: "I am sorry to hear that Daniel will have to be under a doctor's care for some little time. I have no doubt that his condition will straighten out. When it does, we will be happy to have him back with us."

Dan never put himself under a doctor's care, never picked up his prescriptions, never went back to college. He left without telling anyone where he was going.

IN THOSE SAME years, Abraham Myerson was carrying on a correspondence with the publisher Alfred Knopf. In 1931, Knopf had suggested that Myerson write a book. At the outset, they were formal with one another.

> Dear Mr. Knopf,
>
> Your letter of the tenth of December has remained unanswered, largely because I have been formulating in my mind a book for which I have gathered a good deal of material over many years and which, in a sense, represents my mature point of view and is a sort of opus magnum.
>
> The book would center around what I call "the illusion of individuality" ... it can easily be shown that there stream through each individual the materials of the environment and that foodstuffs, gases, rays of light, and energy waves pass in and out of him continually ... As a man eats, he incorporates within himself Nebraska, China, India, and the thousand and one places from which the foodstuffs come, and in a larger sense, incorporates, within himself the sun, and possibly an almost infinite sources of energy ... There is a veritable stream of feeling from man to man, so that the "illusion of individuality" reaches its height in the belief of an individual that he is separate from the rest of mankind ...
>
> As a busy practitioner of medicine it will be impossible for me to devote much consecutive time to this book. I will not be able to get it ready before the end of the summer.
>
> Very sincerely yours,
>
> A. Myerson

If this book were an old movie, we'd cut to time passing with the image of a desk calendar, its leaves blowing back in the wind until—thirteen years later—the date reaches November, 1943, and still Knopf hasn't lost patience. For all writers, this must be construed as an encouraging moment.

> Dear Myerson,
>
> Well, papa, here's that horrid man around again. What's happening to the book? I suppose I know the answer—nothing at all—but I'm a glutton for punishment. So tell me the bad news.
>
> Yours always,
>
> Alfred A. Knopf

December 7, 1943

Dear Knopf,

This "papa" business would be all right if you were a dame instead of a grizzled veteran (my wife says you aren't grizzled) of many publishing campaigns. However, it may interest you to know that I now have a literary secretary and thus it is perfectly possible that I can be pushed into writing the book. My intentions are strictly honorable ... Since you are the guy that might publish it if (my wife says "when") I write it, here's the plan. Since my father and I discussed man in his many aspects of Homo biogiens, Homo sensualis, Homo ferociens, Homo ambivalens, etc. etc., the chapter headings will correspond to these terms, winding up in a great flurry of trumpets and inspiring bugle calls in the final chapter to be entitled Homo gregariens or Psychopathic Society.

[*Author's note: Myerson's father had been a schoolteacher in Lithuania, immigrating to the United States in 1886 where he became a junkman. Myerson worked for his father in his early years when father and son hauled junk and perhaps discussed philosophy.*]

I think I will begin the book with the question: "What is man?" and end with the sentence: "This is man." Now the book is all written, you see. I have the beginning and the end. All I have to do is put some 100,000 or so words in between.

Best wishes,

Abe Myerson

Still no book, but by then they had by become Abe and Alfred to one another.

November 14, 1947

Dear Abe,

I am disappointed in not having had any reply to my letter of November 11th. Would it be possible for you to lunch with me on Friday, the 21st?

Yours sincerely,

Alfred

November 17, 1947

Dear Alfred,

I am sorry to have delayed an answer to your letter, but the fact is that I have been quite ill and have reached the stage where I can only do a part-time job at my office, and the rest of the time I spend in and around the bed ... If you can find time to come over to 33 Taylor Crossway, we should be very happy to entertain you and talk to you on any matter which is on your mind. If the "Malachamovis," which is my way of writing the Hebrew word for Angel of Death, does not flutter his wings too soon, I will have more time for a book ...

Yours sincerely,

A. M.

In September of that year, the Angel made his visit. Abraham Myerson died, his writings later edited by his daughters-in-law and published by Knopf as *Speaking of Man*.

WHEN DAN LEFT college, he hitchhiked through the South, visiting Civil War battlefields. He went to Shiloh and Antietam, with their unfathomable numbers of casualties, to Gettysburg, with its more than one thousand monuments and tablets honoring those who had died. He must have looked at these markers of men who had fought as he had not and known his own inadequacy. But then he looked at the evidence of carnage and knew the world for what it was, senseless.

It showed itself to be senseless—at least in hindsight—when in 1949 Egas Moniz was awarded the Nobel Prize in Medicine for his discovery of lobotomy. At the award ceremony, neurosurgeon Herbert Olivecrona praised Moniz's achievement: "Prefrontal leucotomy must be considered one of the most important discoveries ever made in psychiatric therapy because through its use a great number of suffering people and total invalids have recovered and have been socially rehabilitated." Carl Skottsberg, president of the National Academy of Sciences, also praised the work of Moniz during the ceremonial banquet, calling the first Portuguese laureate "a wonderful man, a famous scientist, a writer of historical books, a politician, statesman, and diplomat, all in one person." As for Moniz's operation, Skottsberg remarked, "Today his method is practiced everywhere with very good results."

After the ceremony, Walter Freeman kissed Moniz on the cheek; as their cheeks touched, Moniz whispered to him, "Mon cher, mon maître." Freeman had to bend down because by then Moniz was a paraplegic, wounded by a schizophrenic patient who had burst into his office and shot him. "I knew at the fifth shot that I was being attacked," Moniz later wrote. "I arose as well as I could and he shot me twice more. Realizing that my right hand was severely injured, I tried to hit him in the head with the inkstand."

TO THE PUBLIC, the Nobel was the equivalent of a Good Housekeeping Seal of Approval, a guarantee that the product worked; if not, the magazine would replace it or refund the purchase price. But no replacement is available for irrevocably damaged brains.

No refund can compensate. Between 1936 and 1949, more than 10,000 lobotomies were performed in the United States. After the Nobel, the number quickly jumped to 18,000; in the United States alone, more people were lobotomized in the three years after the prize than in the previous fourteen years.

RECENTLY I TRACKED down Alexandra Adler's 1927 book *Guiding Human Misfits*, a book that Dan didn't know existed when I told him about it recently. I found words that were true for both of us: "there is one fact always present: if a psychosis occurs in a family, parents always fear that their offspring may also become psychotic."

I look at a photograph of my mother and Phil, Pauline's boy, and they seem happy, normal, sweet. And they were.

And they were not. My mother and aunts had watched as Bennie's illness took over their own mother, leaving them only each other. They learned a lesson, stitched like a sampler on their minds: To Be Sick Is To Be Loved. Growing up, they competed with one another for who had the worst migraines. When the children came along, they competed for whose child was sickest. If I had rheumatic fever, which I did, Pauline's son had to have it too, and an even worse case than mine. To this day, even when I'm verifiably ill, I wonder whether I'm only complying with the family. Throughout my life, I've never known if I'm truly sick—even with something as obvious as a bad cold coming on—or if I'm complying with their expectation that I would need a cold cloth on my forehead.

The problem has been that I've been quite sick, from such undeniable conditions as cancer in my forties. One would think I'd no longer question myself, but I'm adept at inventing new questions—not only Am I sick? but also Did I make this happen?

Friends who know my family history have asked whether I was afraid I'd be mentally ill. More than heredity, it was my family that made me afraid. Never spoken aloud, not even acknowledged to myself, I lived with a sense that I too could be lobotomized.

Well, not really—I dislike turning up authorial screws to make something melodramatic, and besides I was doted on, which brought its own problems.

But yes, really, because Bennie was mute testimony to another kind of doting. Which would prevail? One thing I knew: my mother and aunts could make me ill. It was the air they breathed. It was what they knew: how to take care of the wounded, the blunted, the benumbed.

2.

7.

AFTER THE WAR, ROXBURY'S THREE-DECKERS WERE FILL-
ing up with new people with strange accents; refugees, my mother
explained, who had to leave other countries and come here to us.

Down the street, in an apartment where a room had been
turned into a ballet studio, I took dance classes with Alda Marova,
a curly-haired young woman who was rumored to have danced
with one of the great ballet companies of Russia. Her mother sat
at the piano, foreign in a long black dress, beating out the time as
we little girls tried to rise on point. Practicing at home, I stood at
the door to our living room; my mother dropped a needle onto the
record—*bump bump ba bump bump ba bump*—and on the beat of
the "Waltz of The Flowers," I came whirling into the room.

Then there was Mrs. Landsman, the Polish refugee who
had lost her children in Auschwitz and came to clean our house
once a week, although we didn't have the money to afford a clean-
ing woman and besides, my mother always worked alongside her.
As Mrs. Landsman bent down over a soap bucket, she smelled of
steam and sweat. Later that evening my mother would say, "We
washed the floor with our tears."

It was confusing and exciting; new people were arriving,
we children were dancing, our grownups were crying, and I was
standing on the back porch waiting for my mother to call me in
for dinner.

Out on that back porch something came over me. I called
it THE FEELING, seeing it in my mind's eye in capital letters. It

would begin at the end of the day as I stood out on the porch and watched people across the way come home from work. I felt a grip around my heart, squeezing it. Now I know that it wasn't my heart at all; it was my esophagus. But at six or seven years old, which was when THE FEELING started, I assumed it was my heart because that was the place where feelings happened. I stuck it out as twilight turned to dusk and dusk almost turned to night.

I went back to the kitchen, where my mother was making dinner. She looked at me as she went about adjusting the flame under the pea soup, opening the oven door to check on a leg of lamb my father had brought home from his market. I didn't say anything to her about THE FEELING. I couldn't explain what I felt and besides, I didn't want her to think that I was becoming like Bennie. Already I knew he was the phantom of the family, someone sick who'd been turned into a zombie.

Even though I didn't confess to THE FEELING, my mother must have seen something in my expression night after night that made her decide I needed help. Her fear of Bennie's illness overtaking me was stronger than—than what? Common sense, that might have urged not to react so quickly? But what was good parenting then if not vigilance? Now when parents are keen-eyed to catch a warning glimpse of a child's distress, my mother's recourse would be seen as progressive. But then I didn't understand anything except that maybe something was wrong with me.

One day we took the streetcar together, changing at Grove Hall and getting off at the Arlington Street stop. Walking hand in hand down Marlborough Street, we found the right number of a brownstone; my mother pressed a button on the brass nameplate. We rode up to the doctor's office in a small iron-grilled elevator big enough for only the two of us, a birdcage through which we could see the accompanying sweeping staircase with its Oriental runner that my mother remarked upon. In the waiting room, a loud clock stood ticking on the mantelpiece.

The psychiatrist—recommended, I later learned, by a colleague of the same Abraham Myerson who had recommended

Bennie's lobotomy—is nameless and faceless to me now. But I remember his giving me a pad of paper and a box of crayons and asking me to draw a picture for him. This was exciting; already I had fallen in love with images in a beloved book, *Famous Paintings for Young People*: little Saint Ursula sweetly dreaming under the covers as an angel approaches her canopied bed; St. Francis standing outside a cave in a landscape of golden light, his arms outstretched to receive something glorious that could not be seen. For my subject, I chose a maple leaf, familiar to me because like most New England children I'd scuff through piles of them each autumn. I sketched the leaf's jagged outline, then filled in its central spine and branching veins. Carefully looking through the box, I drew out reds and yellows, shading one color into another. I stopped, considered, then added a touch of flame orange to the pointed tips. As I shaded one color into another, I worried: did the psychiatrist think my choice of subject matter too ordinary, my execution too tame? Lacking imagination? I really did feel like that, although I didn't know those words until much later.

We didn't go back. I never knew why. Was it because we didn't have the money to continue, or had the doctor said that everything was okay, I wasn't sick after all? I was a little sorry because I had been intrigued by his box of forty-eight Crayola crayons, their points standing at attention— Burnt Sienna, Magenta, Pine Green—and the chance they offered to do better.

Back home, I went out to the back porch again, that evening and the ones after, almost as though I were courting THE FEELING. I was being lured by a Blue Violet melancholy, tinged darker now with worry that I would become another Bennie.

I HAD NO idea that anyone had ever felt anything like THE FEEL-ING. But in the mid-1930s, an eight-year-old boy lay in his bed on Haledon Avenue in Passaic, New Jersey, watching the shadows of cars swoop across the ceiling of his room, in awe as one of his biographers has written, "of the immensity of the universe. He would consider the inconceivable distances to the nearest stars and ponder the problems of infinity and the end of space. He was lonely."

I know that little boy, as I know all children who grow up lonely with feelings they have to make sense of by themselves. He was a child surrounded by a gray cloud of mental illness and by the radiant nimbus of his own nature mixed together into a big-eyed, full-lipped, often ecstatic boy who had come up against something he could not understand and could not be protected from. His mother, a teacher, a poet, and a political activist, had been sick for much of her adult life, diagnosed as schizophrenic, in and out of hospitals, eventually treated with electric shock and then with a lobotomy. It was 1947; his parents were divorced, and it fell to the twenty-one-year-old son to sign the papers authorizing the surgery.

Eight years later, about to ship out on a freighter bound for the Bering Strait, the son, Allen Ginsberg, mailed his mother a draft of his new poem, "Howl." Naomi Ginsberg wrote back a letter that clearly showed her diminished self: "this going to the North Pole, who supplies the wearing material? They say when you visit the Eskimos you need a double coat of fur." She wrote of her hallucinations that continued even after the lobotomy: "I still have the wire on my head. The doctors know about it. They are still cutting the flesh & bone."

But the letter also bears the mark of the human being Naomi had been before she became ill. Responding to her son's poem, she wrote: "It seemed to me your wording was a little too hard. Do tell me what father thinks of it." She added a postscript: "I hope you are not taking any drugs as suggested by your poetry. That would hurt me. Don't go for ridiculous things."

The letter was signed, "With love and good news. (mother) Naomi."

THE DAY AFTER writing that letter, Naomi Ginsberg died. Allen didn't return for her funeral. His absence meant that there were not enough men to say Kaddish, the traditional Jewish prayer for the dead. Later he would return to find Naomi waiting for him in his poetry throughout his life, as in *Black Shroud*.

> "I made a mistake" I thought in following the doctors' rules,
> or where'd I get the idea she was screaming and banging
> her head on the wall in neural agony? Was that just my thought
> or hadn't others told me so? Why'd I do it so abrupt
> without consulting the World or the rest of the family—
> Her last look so tranquil and true made me wonder
> why I'd covered her so early with black shroud.
> Had I been insane myself and hasty?"

Had I been insane myself ... that's the question we, the progeny of the lobotomized, ask ourselves. There are other questions raised by Naomi's letter. How had she been able to write it? After forty rounds of electric shock therapy and a radical lobotomy, the person that was Naomi seems to have persisted, responding to her son's poem in part as the teacher, poet, and wife she once had been, and the mother she still was.

What of a person is left after damage to the frontal lobes? In his book *The Executive Brain: Frontal Lobes and the Civilized Mind*, neurologist Elkhonen Goldberg writes that "The lobes are where our humanness resides." But however damaged Naomi's lobes were—and it must have been extensive given that she had one of the relatively early lobotomies—it seems clear to me that she was writing to her son from deep inside a human residence.

YEAR AFTER YEAR, my parents returned to Nantasket Beach, taking me with them, renting a room each summer beginning in the mid-forties. Nantasket then was a world of Jews, of restaurants serving slabs of rare roast beef surrounded by thick white fat, of women in orchid bathing suits walking at the ocean's edge, scanning the sand for friends, waving and walking up to visit one another on blankets where plastic containers filled with fruit salad were on offer.

I was so happy there.

I stayed in the water for hours, sitting on a ridged sandbar where little waves lapped around me. I walked in the sand, looking down for tiny holes that marked the mouths of clams. Taking an outdoor shower at the end of the day, I reveled in placing my wet feet on concrete so that I would leave behind a trail of flat-footed prints. I was without fear; Nantasket was a Bennie-free zone.

On Saturday nights, my father would close up his grocery store and drive out to find us on the porch, waiting for him with a bowl of cut-up watermelon. On Sunday afternoons, we would go to Paragon Park, an amusement park filled with rides. When I was very little my father would lift me up so that I could look through a high window at the roller skaters as they circled an indoor rink, their feet invisible, seeming to glide in the air. He'd buckle me into one of the little cars of the Caterpillar ride that, when coupled with others became a segmented body going up and down the rails, all the children scared and thrilled when a curved canopy would rise up and cover us larvae in green darkness.

When I was a little older, I went alone on my favorite ride, The Red Mill. My mother and father stayed behind a turnstile while I waited on a wooden platform for a boat to splash in. A boatman standing upright at one end—most likely a young kid working a summer job, but to me an almost mythic presence—held out an oar to halt the boat coming in and let the passengers clamber out. I hopped down, and soon I was sitting side by side on planks with strangers, all of us waiting for the boatman to lean forward and give the boat a big push.

We glided into a channel so narrow I could reach out and

touch its rough wood walls. We went on in darkness, water lapping against the sides of the boat, the boat bumping against walls then swinging back to right itself, light coming in only where there was a thin opening between boards. Ahead a faint illumination grew brighter. A diorama came into view hollowed out from the wall; Sleeping Beauty, life-sized, outstretched in a glass coffin, alluring in her prettiness, scary as death, her hands clasping a dusty red velvet rose.

We went past her quietly, swinging back again into the dark until another glimmer of light grew larger and we saw an immense papier mâché figure lying on his back. Tiny figures were binding him with ropes around his ankles. Gulliver's white-irised, black-dotted eyes stared straight up to the ceiling helpless against the swarm.

Darkness again, and then there was an opening into daylight, ahead of us the white struts of a low roller coaster. The boat became a little car chugging up to the summit where we paused for a split second. I waved down to my parents below. They waved back, big smiles on their faces, happy to give me the delights of an ordinary childhood. The car teetered at the top, turned back into a boat and swooped down a water chute, arriving at the platform with great flourishes of water spraying up on either side. I clambered out and we went off to other rides, to silver painted airplanes swinging wider and wider from a center pole.

BUT IN THE dark, behind me, lay Gulliver in his crude diorama, entombed, his huge inert body crinkled in papier mâché, unable to do anything but suffer the demons that attacked him. In my mind, the water rushed back, returning me to Bennie. In those dark channels of my mind—hidden places no one else could see—I had been imprinted with the feeling of his hand behind my ear, and sadness too at his imprisonment. Bennie was there even if he wasn't there.

But I was beginning to realize I had a kind of power. I could make a connection between a character in a storybook and my scary uncle, and then to a story I myself could write one day. I could turn my fate to something other than sickness.

WALTER FREEMAN ACKNOWLEDGED there was a price to be paid: "Every patient probably loses something by this operation, some spontaneity, some sparkle, some flavor of the personality."

But placed against that loss was a greater value. In a cartoon from the early days of promoting the operation, a "Before" drawing depicts a huge brain sitting on the head of a cowering man bound in chains. In the "After" drawing, his chains have fallen to the ground and the man stands upright, smiling happily. The caption reads, "The surgeon's blade, slicing through the connections between the prefrontal areas, frees the patient." Free—that was the rhetoric of lobotomy; it frees the patient, it frees the family. Freedom from constraint placed lobotomy firmly within the ideology of post-war America: with effort and ingenuity, we can be freed of anything that stands in our way.

But time and technology stood in Freeman's way; it took too long to drill into a patient's skull. How to do it in such a way that it did not require those holes? Freeman had an idea: everything could be performed by one individual administering a simple stab through the back of an eye socket directly into the brain. There would be nothing to set up. The patient would be left with nothing worse than black eyes and a splitting headache—plus the usual effects. It would be very easy, very fast and very cheap.

Not a surgeon himself, Freeman had also grown impatient at having to be a bystander. He began to do transorbital lobotomies upstairs in the office, keeping it a secret from his surgical partner, James Watts. One day Watts walked in and saw Freeman leaning over an unconscious patient slumped in a chair with an icepick sticking out from above his eye. Freeman looked up and asked Watts to hold the ice pick so that he could photograph the patient. Watts refused.

Freeman failed to see why people found this new method horrible, especially when he used his preferred tool. With his single-focused pragmatism, he responded that it was the most efficient one for the purpose, so why not use it? Once, he showed a film of an icepick lobotomy to a high school audience. Five students fainted; later he would say, "I'm as good as Frank Sinatra in getting young people to faint."

Freeman decided to go it alone. He had to. Several of his medical colleagues denounced the new icepick method as barbarous. He undertook a crusade to prove his critics wrong. Traveling throughout the United States in a van he dubbed the Lobotomobile, he became a kind of Johnny Appleseed, rolling into town, a scalpel in his pocket and an icepick in his van. Like an itinerant preacher, he'd tout the wonders of lobotomy, urging the townspeople to bring him their difficult relatives, their wayward children, their juvenile delinquents. Across America, mothers and fathers, sisters and brothers, brought their troublemakers—or those they viewed as such—petty criminals, misfits, the retarded, homosexuals, people who didn't fit in—to Freeman's lobotomobile, where they entered as complex human beings and left eerily emotionless.

FREEMAN, EVEN MORE than most of us, exemplified contradictions: wanting to help suffering people, he was ruthless; wanting to uphold his profession, he was unscrupulous; wanting to serve, he put his own glory first; wanting to become famous for finding a cure for mental illness, he achieved notoriety, even called a lunatic by some of his peers. One cannot reckon with nor reconcile this man; believe me, I've tried.

I sent away to his archives at George Washington University for a copy of his unpublished autobiography. I hoped to find the testament of a man grappling with his life. When I came to his account of a trip on which he combined a medical meeting in San Francisco with a disastrous camping excursion to Yosemite, I knew it was not to be.

Hiking up to Vernal Falls with his sons, Freeman reached the place where the Merced River surges over a cliff and drops steeply to sharp boulders below. He discovered that he hadn't brought enough water. Keen, his eleven-year-old son, walked to the waterfall's edge to fill his canteen. He slipped on a rock and plunged into the river. A sailor standing nearby vaulted over the railing, but he too was swept away. At the one moment when hyperactive Freeman should have acted, he stood a distance away "as if I had become paralyzed. The last look I had was Keen's face as he went over the edge." Freeman never mentions Keen again other than to lament the loss of a potentially good surgeon ("he had a surgeon's hands") noting only that on his return home, he exchanged his camper for a Cadillac.

In his Lobotomobile, side by side with his camping equipment, was an electroconvulsive shock box, Freeman's preferred method to quiet a patient before operating. He said that electric shock was faster and cheaper than anesthesia, even though his patients suffered broken bones from convulsions. At the risk of being overly Freudian myself, I wonder whether his sadism—undeniable I think—was traceable in part to an incident in his childhood. When Walter was caught playing truant, he expected that his father would apply a switch to his backside; instead, his father opened his desk, took out the multi-tailed whip known as a cat-o'-nine-tails, and while Walter watched, flogged his own back until it was bloody.

What would be the impact of such a scene on a young boy? The message was, at one level, clear: I am your father, your wrongdoing will hurt me, I shall be the one to suffer for your sins, and no expiation will ever be forthcoming. Was Freeman left with a desire to do good so that his father would never have to suffer again? So that he himself would be given the sweet strokes of appreciation? Was he also left with the desire to punish, to do wrong so that he his father would go on hurting himself? That young man, sitting beside Moniz at the 1935 Second International Neurological Congress was, I think, unaware of the strangely mixed messages, both placating and antagonistic, speeding from his limbic system to his very own frontal lobes.

On one five-week summer trip, Freeman drove eleven thousand miles in the Lobotomobile, keeping a log of the number of operations he performed at each stop: Mendocino, California, nine; Lincoln, Nebraska, eight; Little Rock, Arkansas, four, ... noting also four deaths from the surgery. As the townspeople said of the Lone Ranger as he galloped off into the distance: Who was that man?

Freeman drove on, making a world of people who could not feel.

HE GOT TO the point where he could perform a lobotomy in twelve minutes. It was almost as though his patients were coming to him on an assembly line. The sociologist Max Weber, born some thirty years before Freeman, wrote, "Precision, speed, unambiguity, knowledge of the files, continuity, discretion, unity, strict subordination, reduction of friction and of material and personal costs—these are raised to the optimum … the objective discharge of business primarily means a discharge of business according to calculable rules and 'without regard for persons.'"

Without regard for persons—this to me is the key that connects lobotomy with the story of people considered not good enough to live as complex human beings. The designation of the supposedly "unfit" has always been with us, but in the twentieth century it has been organized through the social policy of eugenics and the massive ethnic cleansing that was the Holocaust. The label of unfit has given a rationale in a deadly continuum to belittle, to take away value from people in the eyes of others and in their own eyes, to humiliate them, to excise their essential humanity, and to exterminate them. Hannah Arendt wrote that the most difficult problem for the perpetrators of the Final Solution was "how to overcome … the animal pity by which all normal men are affected in the presence of physical suffering." The twentieth century provided far too many ways to solve the problem. One was the elimination of all feelings.

The lunacy went on: Catholic theologians debated whether a person should be accepted into the priesthood after a lobotomy. The issue came down to free will; the Pope implied that an operation that made a Catholic an automaton by removing free will would be unlawful, but the church did not object to some diminution of personality.

WHY WAS THERE no outcry, no call for mercy?

Peacetime was about expansion, of businesses and families; it was not a time to call a halt to yet more expansion. Also, the mad were disruptions at a time that had hung out a Do Not Disturb sign.

A few people spoke out: in 1949, *Newsweek* reported that psycho-analyst and director of the New York Psychiatric Institute Nolan D. C. Lewis said, "It disturbs me to see the number of zombies that these operations turn out ... I think it should be stopped before we dement too large a section of the population." But dissent was quashed by the looming authority of the Nobel.

Were Walter Freeman to read this, he'd be outraged; he believed he was helping people, his confidence bolstered by the reception he received at state hospitals where the superinten-dents encouraged him to lobotomize as many patients as he could. Lobotomy kept costs down; the upkeep of an insane patient cost the state $35,000 a year while a lobotomy cost $250, after which the patient could be discharged. Freeman drove across America waving his slogan: "Lobotomy sends them home."

Thanksgivings, 1950 and onward

WE WERE ALL there, the feeling and the unfeeling, the old getting older and the young getting older too, the indulged who ate and the helpful who worked, the good cheer and the fake cheer, the closeness and the pettiness, the present and its portents, the expanding and the diminishing, the so-called normal alongside the zombie on the couch, all the axes on which my family lived and embraced one another and sacrificed its own.

Each year we gathered at a cousin's house for Thanksgivings, days that stretched over years but felt almost as though they were one long day, each varying so slightly that the times spun together into a rapid succession of barely moving images. The day began with my father driving first to pick up Jen, then to Roxbury to pick up Bennie and my grandmother. My mother went up the apartment stairs to fetch her mother and brother. Through the glass pane in the front door, I saw them coming down, first my mother's pumps, then my grandmother's little white-laced shoes, followed by Bennie's brown clodhoppers. When he reached the sidewalk, Bennie began to twirl. My mother put her hand on his forearm like a brake and steered him into the back seat.

We drove out to Lexington, past the statue of the Minuteman on the Commons. Jen tamped out a Winchester cigarette from her gold mesh case, flicked her lighter and inhaled, rolling down a window and asking, "Do you mind?" We went past the farm that sold pumpkins and sheaves of Indian corn in the subtler colors of that never-forgotten big Crayola box: Indigo. Red-orange. Goldenrod. When we pulled up at my cousin's split-level house, my mother went over to Bennie's side and took his arm. Jen tucked her mother's hand into the fold of her elbow. Together the sisters shepherded their mother and brother across the new November ice, thin and crackly.

At the door to the brightly lit house, my mother called back to my father, "Be careful, it's slippery."

We were a sliding procession, my father holding the pot of squash and me holding onto him. Minna was waiting at the door.

With raised eyebrows, she silently queried my mother: *Helen, is everything all right?* My mother nodded yes, then gestured with her chin in the direction of the kitchen, signaling to Minna that she was about to help with dinner and Minna should take over with Bennie.

"How nice you look, Bennie. Is that a new bowtie?" Minna asked as she slipped Bennie's coat off his shoulders. She guided him to the couch, where he sat with his feet planted on the rug, hands on his thighs. Jen went over and sat on the arm of the couch, offering her small stock of conversation, mostly about her store. When Bennie didn't respond—he never did, she never expected him to—she'd light a cigarette, inhale, pat his shoulder and move off to talk business with Sam.

Francie was in the kitchen, her chosen place where she could be capable and hidden. She was engaged in the delicate task of unmolding the bombe, an annual dessert made of sliced Twinkies interleaved with ice cream, packed into a domed pan and kept in the freezer for several days. She ran a knife around the rim of the pan and placed a platter over the top, flipping the dome right-side up and lightly tapping the metal with her knuckles. Tap. Tap.

When I picture that Thanksgiving dining room table, it is in the gorgeous Technicolor of 1950s films: bright green peas with little onions in a cut glass dish; rosy applesauce (the secret was cinnamon hearts); heaped orange squash that my parents had boiled the day before, taking turns mashing; sweet and sour meatballs studded with raisins; Jell-O molds glowing like stained glass, mandarin oranges suspended in deep ruby red.

The sisters walked around the buffet, my mother filling a plate for Bennie, carrying it to him and tucking a napkin into his shirt collar, cutting the turkey breast and offering it to his pouchy down-turned mouth, Minna filling a plate for her mother.

When it was time for dessert, Francie brought out the bombe, intact and perfectly rounded, greeted with oohs and aahs. She blushed before scooting back to the kitchen. Then it was Jen's turn to go around the table and fill a plate for Bennie, this time with Toll House cookies, brownies with walnuts, a slice of the bombe over which she spooned hot fudge sauce. Bennie surveyed the offerings. Then, swiftly and silently, he picked up a chunk of something in his pudgy hand and tried to swallow it whole.

"Chew, Bennie," Jen said. "It won't go down that way."

Pauline and her husband George would drop by after an earlier dinner with friends and business associates. They were people with other lives, other responsibilities, living on the North Shore in a town twenty minutes up the coast from Boston but seen by her sisters as halfway to the moon. They were presidents, respectively, of their synagogue's Sisterhood and Brotherhood, those pillars of Jewish community life in which "sister" and "brother" take on expansive meanings beyond one's own family.

Pauline entered the room in a soft cloud of excitement, something special in her arms for Bennie, wrapped and tied with decorative ribbons.

Bennie took it in his hands.

"Open it, Bennie," Minna urged. She helped him undo the wrapping, exclaiming enthusiastically at a new pair of gloves, or a warm scarf. Later she would tell my mother that Bennie didn't need those things but she couldn't bring herself to tell Pauline that he had enough gloves, enough scarves. Besides, Pauline had her own ideas about what she should bring. She brought string-tied bakery boxes of pecan and pumpkin pies. It was a little late for another dessert, but the pies were served anyway.

"These are good, Pauline," my father said, sampling both.

"Where did you get them?" my mother asked, implying she might want to buy them someday.

After Pauline and her husband left, Minna, Helen, Jen, and Francie compared notes. Had Pauline gained a little weight? Was her son Phil really sick as she had said, or was he spending the day with his snooty North Shore friends? Were the piecrusts too thick, the pumpkin filling a little too spicy? Besides, my mother sniffed, everything else was homemade.

My mother didn't ordinarily snipe but she was still hurting

from a wound that Pauline had inflicted on her more than thirty years ago.

"Each week," my mother told me, "I put aside money from my paycheck so that Pauline could have pearls on her white kid gloves for her wedding. I would have stolen for her without a second thought, that's how much I loved her. But when she made her own friends, it was as though I never existed."

Pauline has said that my mother never reciprocated her own love, that in recent years she had made a phone call to tell my mother that she still loved and missed her. According to Pauline, my mother said, "What's the point in bringing this up all over again? What's done is done. It's over."

But can sisterly love be over? I don't think so, but it can be damaged.

AS SOON AS I was old enough, I took a walk after Thanksgiving dinner in the cold New England air, past blue smoke coming from chimneys and television screens flickering through the slats of Venetian blinds. I strode, hands in my pockets, rejoicing in having escaped from the too-hot house and into my own thoughts. I was beginning to know that walking alone would one day lead to a different life.

If Dan were there at those Thanksgivings he'd join me on my walks, both of us taking deep breaths of the cold air. I once asked him what he did when he came home from his trip to the Civil War sites. "I lived at home," he said, "and holed up in my room. I read. I wanted to start with *The Odyssey* and work my way up, but then I heard about this fellow James Joyce and that was it for me." Dan and I shared a lust for self-improvement. I had found a list of One Hundred Best Books in a magazine and began to read them at a two-week Jewish summer camp. When the counselor came to round us up for something I didn't want to do, I'd crouch on a toilet lid in the bathroom stall, balancing myself while reading *Babbitt*.

Dan was showing me that other kinds of escape were possible; he was living then in a basement apartment on Beacon

Hill with his redheaded girlfriend, later to become his wife. A set designer, she painted scenes of Paris on their windowshades; at night they were no longer in Boston but surrounded by sidewalk cafes, easels, the Eiffel Tower.

On one of those Thanksgiving walks, I remember his saying about the family, "They drive me nuts."

"Me too," I said, "but it's Bennie who gives me the creeps."

"He's harmless," Dan said. "It's all the others you should worry about."

Coming back to the house, we would enter to a chorus of Where Were You? Your Mother Was So Worried.

The procession of leaving was underway: my mother leading Bennie, aunts and uncles walking gingerly, carrying tinfoil-covered pots to their cars. I joined them, holding our pot with its leftover squash.

On the way back, our car was filled with well-fed quiet, leavened with a bit of relief. We drove along Route 2, beside the slushy Charles River, past the spare clapboard houses of Brighton, under the elevated train tracks, to Roxbury. When we pulled up at the curb, my mother got out of the car to help Bennie, but before she could get to his side he let himself out and began to twirl on the sidewalk, our family dervish whirling in his own slow trance, a bludgeoned brother swimming through our family's undercurrents.

IN THOSE YEARS, Harry was coming home each night to Francie's casseroles after spending long days working at a relative's carpet store. He was content to sit in their by-now-somewhat-shabby living room paging through magazines that Minna brought over after she'd finished reading them, *Reader's Digest* for Harry, with its humorous "Life in These United States" anecdotes, *Ladies Home Journal* for Francie, with its advice columns and kitchen-tested recipes. They may not have been happy exactly, and Francie still had her troubles, but the seven years since they'd been back from Reno had been relatively placid.

JEN LOST MOE. He had got tired of the affair—the secrecy, and frankly, now that he was older, the sex didn't seem as important. It was as a partner in The Emily Rose Shoppe that he wanted to continue his relationship with Jen. He brought his adult son into the business, a smart move—his son was a go-getter, like Moe himself. Jen must have agreed to the arrangement, but the infiltration of Moe's family into her world of the Emily Rose Shoppe could not have pleased her.

She had moved away from Roxbury to an apartment in Brookline, a town just beyond Boston's city limits that figured in my family's aspirations as a promised land where even the grocery stores carried a better class of peaches and asparagus. Jen understood the lineaments of raising herself up; she hired a decorator who surrounded her with Persian rugs, paintings of Roman street scenes, lamps made of Czech glass with delicate hanging crystals cut into facets. I was fascinated by those prisms; I would tap them with my index finger and set them to swinging lightly, one against another, wanting to hear the small sound of clinking.

Jen didn't talk about Moe. Instead she surprised the family by getting engaged to a timid man who seemed to materialize out of the proverbial nowhere, nice enough but nowhere near Jen's sophistication. Her sisters were appalled. They knew she was making a mistake and tried to talk her out of it. The husbands were more sanguine. "Let her make her own mistakes," they said.

Jen was betting that Moe would be jealous and want her back. She lost the bet. In the store's basement where they used to make love, he told her once and for all that it was over. To spite him, she married her fiancé; a year later, she divorced him. Always dissatisfied, mostly with herself, Jen had her hairdresser dye her hair a different color from month to month: ash, honey, copper, platinum. She bought expensive shoes in shops far more elegant than her own, so many pairs that it upset her sisters who knew Jen didn't really want the shoes themselves, only their promise of being the right thing. But when she'd try them on at home, she thought they didn't look good on her. She'd begin her requests to Minna with, "Would you mind bringing these back … ?" Minna could never say no. Besides, it was easy. Minna and Sam too had moved to Brookline, close to Coolidge Corner, within walking distance of Jen's apartment.

COOLIDGE CORNER IN those years, and later when I was growing up, was an odd hybrid of a Brahmin Boston—where dowagers put aside cases of port at S. S. Pierce to be bestowed on their grandsons when they entered Harvard—side by side with an intimate Jewish world where Jack and Marion presided over a fabled eponymous delicatessen that featured huge sandwiches that, when eaten in their entirety, qualified the eater for inclusion among names listed on a wall as members of the Fressers' (Yiddish for glutton) Fraternity. It was a world of Pick-A-Chick, Lady Grace, and Cyreld, the latter a shop owned by a semi-mythic woman who was supposed to design couture dresses. It was considered a coup to have seen Cyreld herself, back from Paris in her rose-lipsticked, black-chignoned flesh.

For both old and newer residents, Coolidge Corner was like a traditional village where people had their lineages, as I learned when I went to my mother's dentist, who said, "I knew your grandmother and your poor Uncle Bennie." Being known has its advantages: like a net thrown over its inhabitants, familiarity provides a sense of safety. One's dramas could be played out on a small stage.

Later, even though the net continued to keep me in its loosening meshes, I saw that the stage may have been small but the dramas were not. In his 1949 essay "Tragedy and the Common Man," Arthur Miller wrote, "In this age few tragedies are written. For one reason or another, we are often held to be below tragedy— or tragedy above us ... I believe that the common man is as apt a subject for tragedy in its highest sense as kings were."

In our dramas as in our comedies, in our lobotomies as in our fressers, my family would come to know that truth firsthand.

WITH MOE NO longer available as an outlet for Jen's fierce energy, she began to focus its beam on Francie.

"She's alone all day; that's not good for her," Jen said to my mother.

"If Francie got herself out of the house," my mother said, "she wouldn't be alone."

Jen kept fretting.

"Francie needs nicer things," Jen said to Minna. "She and Harry should come live with me."

"Let her alone for God's sake," my mother said.

For my mother there was little satisfaction in the daily round of family, no interest in phone call after phone call, Minna "stirring the pot," as my mother used to say to me.

"You think Minna is so wonderful. I don't want to disillusion you but …" She stopped herself, suppressing what she had about to say, perhaps for my benefit.

No, I thought, I won't believe you, you're just jealous of my closeness with Minna.

My mother *was* jealous, but now I think that what she wanted to say was that Minna made trouble with her endless pot stirring. It was a way to not let anyone get away.

After yet another call from Minna about Jen or Francie, my mother would hang up the phone and turn to me, crying in aggravation: "Can't my sisters leave me alone for one second?"

8.

"HELP, BENNIE IS BEING FRESH."

It was my grandmother phoning late at night. My parents spoke in low voices that I strained to overhear, my ear poked up from under the bedcovers.

"Being fresh ... " What, I wondered, did that mean? I guessed that my grandmother's phone call was about something forbidden because there was a surreptitious quality to the whispered exchange between my parents. Later it dawned on me that Bennie must have had sexual eruptions, not unusual it turns out in cases of extreme frontal lobe damage.

After a call from my grandmother, my father drove back to Roxbury, where he helped the caretaker propel Bennie to bed, calmed my grandmother and returned home to not enough sleep. He had to get up early and go to work the next day, which was every day, seven days a week. We were worried: there was a rumor that an Elm Farms supermarket would be moving next door to our small market. The store was our livelihood, our limited lease on security. So far, it hadn't expired.

By then, we too had moved away from Roxbury, not making it all the way to Brookline but to nearby Brighton, where we rented a first floor apartment in a two-family house. Life was expanding for the sisters, the circle no longer as exclusive as it had been. My mother made interesting friends. One of them spoke French and had clothes made for her in Hong Kong. Once I caught a glimpse of her elegantly ordered lingerie drawer, rows of lace bras, a grid of nylon stockings each rolled and turned outward like flowers, a vision of luxe and self-regard.

Across the street from our new apartment was a monastery. I'd walk up the hill to Saint Gabriel's, nervous that I might commit a Jewish heresy were I to meet a priest and greet him as "Father." But I'd go anyway, with my writing notebook and drawing pad, joyful among rows of orchard trees and carefully tended vegetable gardens. Years later when I saw images of sowing in *Le Très Riche Heures du Duc de Berry*, I was happy to recognize a place I'd known.

When I was eleven, I took a test and was accepted to Girls Latin School, a public school for smart girls, all of us studying Latin and Greek below busts of Cicero and Caesar, their blank eyes staring ahead. Rich or poor, proud or ashamed, none of it mattered so long as we could translate their words. Latin still had the respect it had when Minna reprinted in her *Circle News* an article from the *Boston Traveler*: "Latin makes for culture and culture is a main factor in making a nation great. Culture is refinement; it bridges the gap between the savage and the civilized."

I thrived. Our books spread out in front of us with their glossy numeraled plates, a gravure of cypresses bordering the Appian Way to its vanishing point. We sent our secret words across the aisle: *semper ubi sub ubi* ("always wear underwear"). I was the first seventh grader ever to win the school-wide poetry award given by the school's literary magazine. I can still feel my heart leaping when I walked up the central aisle of the auditorium to accept my prize. I wanted to hold out my own hands and say, "Here, this is what I love; it stands for me, for my own self. Know it and you will know me."

Or at least a partial me, enthralled by beauty but knowing that to admit to my dark and light shadings might lead me straight back to the psychiatrist. I revealed even less a few years later when my parents moved to Brookline, disqualifying me from attending Boston Girls Latin. In my new school it was important to fit in. When I carried a book whose cover might reveal that I was a "brain," I hid it under my jacket.

1953

IN THE DINING room of that Brighton apartment with its French Provincial wallpaper, its breakfront displaying my mother's collection of china with the cracked parts turned to the wall, a candelabra in the center of the table with a basin spilling over with artificial grapes, Francie would help to set the table. An image, virtually cinematic, comes to my mind: Francie's freckled forearm over my shoulder, her hand putting down a plate.

Harry and Francie visited us often there. I was turned off by Harry's white skin, soft jowls, his overly friendly manner in which self-loathing was evident.

"What's the matter, kid, you can't stand me?"

Pause.

"I don't blame you."

After dinner, Harry and my dad would unfold a card table and settle in to play cribbage, speaking the game's patois, "his nibs" when the Jack was the starter card. Most of the time they were quiet, intent on the long black board. When one would score points, he'd gleefully move a peg along a row to a further hole. Standing behind my father, looking down at the table, I didn't understand the game, but I enjoyed the easy, uncomplicated camaraderie of men.

Sometimes Francie would stand behind Harry for a few seconds. Harry would reach up to put an arm around her waist. She'd turn her head to one side and pull away from him, but with a tiny smile and a dry chuckle as if to admit she liked it.

JEN TOOK FRANCIE and Harry out to dinner at a restaurant in Chinatown where she and Moe had been regulars, settling the two of them in a red vinyl booth under fringed paper lanterns. Sitting across from them, Jen did the ordering, choosing dishes she thought they'd like: chow mein, sweet and sour chicken, egg foo young.

The waiter knew Jen from past visits. He brought over dishes covered by domes that he lifted with a flourish, steam rising, briefly hiding the three of them from one another.

"I have something I want to talk about with the two of you," Jen said as she spooned food onto each of the plates. Being direct was the wrong tack to take, but Jen wasn't subtle.

Harry and Francie exchanged the secret look of people who have been married for twelve years and share a suspicion that something is up.

"I've been thinking, it would be better if you moved in with me," Jen said. "I have that extra bedroom I don't use. You could have your own bathroom and you wouldn't have to worry about rent. I'd like to have you close to me."

Francie heard Jen's moderate tone of voice and understood that it masked the force behind it. She said nothing.

Harry began to sputter, the loose skin of his cheeks shaking. He attempted to protest, his voice a spurting faucet:

"But—"

Jen quickly turned him off. "Don't say anything now," she said in a placating tone. "There's no hurry. Go home and talk about it."

JEN HAD SAID, "No hurry" to Francie and Harry, but that wasn't her nature. She was impatient, a boxer who leaves the ring just long enough to put ice on a split lip, then comes out swinging.

Perhaps Jen had to be a slugger; a successful businesswoman in a man's world couldn't afford the time to analyze her motives. She did what she knew how to do—provide, for her mother, for Bennie, for Francie, even for Dan when he needed money to realize his dream of opening a theater. When a new dress line came into the store, she brought home styles she thought would look good on Francie, holding them up on her as though she were a mannequin in a shop window.

The material world held particular allure for Jen and my mother, although not for Minna, whose basic style was lavender blouses and lace-up oxfords. Jen lent my mother clothes, fancy things my mother could never buy for herself, a broadcloth swing coat lined with chinchilla that was an object of my desire. I lay my girl cheek against the fur, such dark softness against my skin.

JEN DIDN'T GIVE up her pursuit. There was no time limit, no cut-off, but she pressed as hard as she could on the next day and the next.

In the privacy of their own apartment, Harry and Francie talked about Jen's offer.

"If this is what you want, kid ... "

Francie replied with a vehemence that surprised them both. "No, Harry. You have to say no to her."

"She's your sister, kid," Harry said. "You've got to be the one to tell her."

Harry got up from the kitchen table to get one of Minna's brownies.

"What's the big deal?" he asked, coming back with two brownies on his plate, "Will the world fall apart because you say no to her?"

If I say no to her, Francie might have thought, Jen will stop loving me.

I wish I could have reassured her—Jen won't stop loving you, maybe she'll even let up.

I do believe Jen couldn't stop loving Francie. Nor was she vengeful. But she could have become distant, and even that would have terrified Francie.

"I can't." There was a plea in Francie's voice. Harry heard it and wanted to be accommodating, not because he felt it was the right thing to do but because it was easier. He felt stuck, in service to a wife who demanded more of his attention than he wanted to give. He was in favor of whatever would buy him the most freedom.

"Talk it over with Minna. She'll help you."

Francie began to weep. Harry went over to her and stroked her forehead.

"Come on, kid, that's it. Let me see you smile."

Francie looked up and tweaked her mouth into a tiny smile. Harry felt glad to have been of use.

NEAT AND ANXIOUS, Francie took the Commonwealth Avenue streetcar to Minna's house. It had been a long time since she'd lived with Minna and Sam, but their house, wherever it was, remained for her a place of refuge.

Minna, apron tied at the back of her thin waist, was baking in preparation for a meeting of her women's club at her house. Between Minna's frequent checks of the oven to see whether a cake had risen, Francie tried to get her attention.

"Don't let Jen make me go there. Say something to her. She listens to you."

One could say that Francie's timing was bad. No time would have been good, but Minna already had a lot on her mind. Sam had been diagnosed with colon cancer; Dan was farther away than ever, in Northern California, where he'd taken a job in broadcasting (although, even if he were closer, she knew he still would stay away from them).

Francie pleaded, "Save me."

Minna wanted to help; it was her nature, but she didn't want to antagonize Jen. It was Jen's money that went on paying for their mother's and Bennie's expenses. The family couldn't do without it. I don't think that Minna really believed Jen would take her money away if she were to be thwarted. It was more that some sort of fragile equilibrium had been achieved, and Minna didn't want to rock the boat.

"Save me," Francie cried.

Minna, the sister who had always been a mother to Francie, turned away.

On the streetcar home, Francie tried not to weep. But then she entered her apartment, cherished because it was hers. I imagine her placing her purse on the hall table, taking off her coat and putting it on a hanger, buttoning the top button so it won't slip off, pulling aside a curtain, pushing open a window and banging her fists against the sill until they were raw and bleeding.

9.

THE GILCHRIST CURTAINS, ONCE LOVINGLY BOUGHT BY my mother and carefully hung in Francie and Harry's apartment, were taken down, folded up, put into boxes, and donated to a Jewish relief agency.

"You won't need them," Jen said. "I have everything."

At Jen's apartment, Francie and Harry were installed in their own bedroom with thick wall-to-wall carpeting and a bed with a tufted headboard.

Jen bought Francie a mink coat.

"What does Jen think she's doing," my mother said to Minna, "buying Francie a mink she doesn't want?"

Francie went along with it, as did Minna and my mother, even though they disapproved. Francie showed neither gratitude nor displeasure, keeping her head down much of the time. Often she took to her bed with migraine headaches.

One night Harry said, "I tell you, Francie, this has to stop."

"Sh sh sh …" Francie huddled under the covers.

"I'm going to say something to her."

Jen was working at her inlaid desk, doing the bookkeeping for the store, her ever-present ashtray beside the desk pad. She looked up, irritated to hear Harry opening the bedroom door, surprised to see him looking as determined as his face could manage.

"I know you mean well, Jen," Harry said, "but don't treat my wife like she's your child."

His jowls were shaking even as he spoke with unexpected force.

Jen remained cool, speaking in her voice that could sound like something scratching against dry timber.

"I don't know what you're talking about, Harry."

"Of course you do—buying her things she doesn't want, things I can't get for her. I'm her husband, how do you think that makes me feel?"

"If I can do it, why shouldn't I? If she doesn't like it, she can come to me about it."

"But she won't, you know that Jen."

"Goodnight, Harry." Jen turned back to her work.

When Harry went back to the bedroom, he wanted to be patted on the back for standing up to Jen but he didn't want Francie to know that his big moment had ended in humiliation. But what he wanted didn't matter; Francie had taken a sedative from the batch she'd been hiding away ever since she'd got that prescription from Reno, forever refillable. When Harry sat down at the edge of the bed and looked over at his wife she was already sleeping.

IN THE POSTWAR forties and fifties, women were asleep. They were not sisters to Sleeping Beauty who, after all, was just waiting to be awakened. These sleeping women were more closely related to the movies of the times—Joan Crawford in *Possessed*, which ends with the protagonist asleep, her disturbance soothed by drugs with the implication that she will awaken becalmed, her spirit broken. These were women who weren't able to stand up for themselves in a world that was making them more and more dependent.

In his prescient book, *The Nervous Housewife*, Abraham Myerson wrote "Every human being is a pot boiling with desires, passions, lusts, wishes, purposes, ideas, and emotions, some of which he clearly recognizes and clearly admits, and some of which he does not clearly recognize and which he would deny."

My family knew about the boiling pot and about not recognizing what was in it.

Myerson went on to say, "People get tired, disgusted, apprehensive; they hate where they should love; love where they should hate; are jealous unreasonably; are bored, tortured by monotony; have their hopes, purposes, and desires frustrated and blocked; fear death and old age, however brave a face they may wear; want happiness and achievement, and some break, one way or another, according to their emotional and intellectual resistance."

Break they did. The first one to shatter was Harry.

AS HARRY ADDED up the scores in the weekly cribbage games, he talked to my dad about his unhappiness, looking toward the kitchen to make sure he wasn't being overheard. My father gave Harry his "This Is How It Is" shrug, implying what's the use of fighting? He'd adopted his own survival strategy: lie low and accommodate himself to the obsessions of his wife and her sisters.

When my father and Harry neared the end of their games, the cribbage board bristled with black pegs. Years later I was reminded of those boards when I saw Kongo fetish figures with nails stuck into them. Harry could have used something that conferred power. Instead he spent his days kneeling on hard floors, measuring strangers' rooms for soft carpeting. When he came back to Jen's, knees aching, he was greeted not with balm but with the hurting silence of a wife who had turned away.

He was on the road now several times a month, going to hick towns, staying in seedy motels, tempted once again by gambling. The money he earned would vanish into thin air but what did it matter? Jen was paying for all their needs. Piss, he would think. He had got what he wanted, a kind of freedom, but he couldn't get Francie out of his head. She had a hold on him. Everything had a hold on him. When he phoned his wife, look what happened—Jen picked up the phone. Sometimes she'd say that Francie was sleeping. Maybe she was, maybe she wasn't, who knows? Let Jen worry about her.

After a while he no longer talked to my father about his problems. He trudged along, a tape measure in his pocket. Alone in motels, he'd lose his fight with himself and drive into town, scouting barren blocks for the lights of a casino.

MINNA LOOKED ON helplessly, aware now that her refusal to help Francie was leading toward tragedy.

She talked it over with my mother, but it wasn't an honest discussion because Minna never told her that Francie had pleaded to be saved from Jen, and that she'd refused to help her. Because Minna was too ashamed of herself to tell the whole story, my mother was under the impression that Francie had never protested but simply gone along with Jen's proposal. Now she said, "Francie made her bed, let her lie in it."

ONE DAY MINNA heard Francie's stunned voice at the other end of the line and knew this was no ordinary phone call. Harry hadn't come home at all, not after work, not at bedtime, not the next morning when his side of the bed was still untouched.

That morning a letter had been dropped off at Jen's door. Francie read it aloud.

Dear Francine,

My son Harold has asked me to write you. He will not be coming back. He can no longer live in such a situation as your sister Jen has made and he cannot live any more with your troubles. Your family is making my Harold sick. Do not try to contact him.

Sincerely,

Mrs. M. Gurstein

What a coward, Minna thought, letting his mother do his business for him. For an instant she thought of Leon, another man who'd let his mother do the deciding. But she didn't say that to Francie. She said she'd be right over. Then she realized she still had cookies in the oven. She slid out the rack, left the cookies to cool, closed the snaps on her Persian lamb coat, hurried out the door then paused, remembering she had to call my mother and see if she could reach Sam—no, something told her to leave it all for later. Go. Now.

I HAD NO idea anything unusual was happening. It was Saturday morning and I was walking along Beacon Street, looking forward to meeting my mother at Jen's and going shopping at nearby Coolidge Corner, maybe getting a red crewneck sweater and a Black Watch plaid skirt like the older high school girls were wearing in the mid-fifties.

The door to Aunt Jen's apartment was open. I walked down the hallway, felt a breeze from an open window. No one was in the living room. I heard a voice, my mother's, on the phone, coming from the back bedroom. I started to walk toward her, but first I had to stop to use the bathroom. The door was closed. I turned the knob.

Blood. In the sink and on the floor, streaks of it on the mirror and the wall tiles.

My mother must have heard me come in because suddenly she was there at the bathroom door, reaching in front of me to close it. She said Francie had tried to hurt herself, she was in the hospital, Minna and Jen were with her. My mother was going there now, I should go home, she'd be there as soon as she could.

I didn't go home. I went to Brigham's where I ate a hot fudge sundae and wondered: My mother knew I was coming to the apartment. Couldn't she have watched out for me, met me at the door, warned me before I saw that bathroom?

I was a young girl, innocent of trying to take a life, unacquainted with blood other than my own. The tin can smell of Francie's blood was strong enough to lodge in me for the rest of my life.

With Francie's suicide attempt, something in me hardened. When I think back to that day, I see myself walking up the street, gay and unafraid, to the accompaniment of "Peter's Theme" from Prokofiev's *Peter and the Wolf.* Then I opened a door and met the wolf. Unlike Peter, I hadn't been able to catch it by the tail. If anything, I was the duck that the wolf swallowed, trapped in the belly of family.

It was the beginning of numbing myself. It would take a very long time after the bloody bathroom to open myself to loving the people who had let me be swallowed.

WHAT HAPPENS TO all the children with our exaltations and pencils? We become numb because we must in order not to be crushed by the brunt of what we must leave behind. And we do have to leave, all the children intent on our own paths. We have to shut off the current of our feelings; otherwise the pain of our families, their betrayals and their love, would overwhelm us.

Alexandra Adler wrote, "It is occasionally observed that children may keep in the back of their minds the knowledge of how to overcome in later life, because of similar experiences which they went through during childhood." The connection that Adler makes between childhood and resilience is a true one, and I am good at overcoming difficulties, but one of the hardest has been to dissolve protective distance, to arrive at a point along the way when we know we are no longer fragile, the point when retrospective love and pity become possible and Allen Ginsberg could write "Kaddish," when we realize no one can take our created selves away from us—not, that is, unless we do it to ourselves, as I would do later.

I think now that our collective DNA is made up of twisted strands of pathology and creation. One is toxic; the other would save us.

10.

WHEN FRANCIE CAME HOME FROM THE HOSPITAL AND got stronger, she pleaded with her sisters to get Harry to come back.

No one knew what to do. Was he waiting to be called back, hoping for an inducement? Might he come back and then leave her again? She couldn't survive that. Might his return be the thing that could save her?

And by the way where was he?

Sam ran into Harry's cousin, a blabbermouth; Harry had gone to New York and was working in a hotel near Times Square.

Now that they knew where he was, the family faced a tough decision: should someone go to New York and try to persuade him to return?

Minna and Sam made plans for a family meeting at Howard Johnson's coffee shop at Coolidge Corner. Pauline chose not to come; she thought Jen had been wrong to try and make Francie and Harry move in with her, but she was staying clear of the front line.

"LET HIM GO," Sam said. "I never want to see his lousy face again."

Minna said, "What if she hurts herself again?"

Jen said she didn't think that Harry would stay away.

This was pure wishful thinking. It hadn't occurred to Jen that Harry had begun to gamble again, that he could be in trouble, that she herself might have to back off before he could even think about returning.

My father, always willing to give someone another chance, offered his own point of view. "Look, he's weak. But who isn't? And he went through a lot. Being married to Francie is no picnic ... "

My mother cast a warning eye at him, an encompassing look that said, "Don't antagonize Sam, you won't win. He'll say you're too soft."

With the blindness of a person who can't afford to understand what she'd set in motion, Jen said, "Should I go?"

As they totaled up the bill and split it, a decision was made. Sam would go. He knew his way around. He wouldn't let Harry get away with anything.

ON HIS WAY to see Harry, Sam walked through Times Square, filled with hookers and winos, over to Forty-third Street, where Harry was working as a night clerk in a seedy hotel.

Sam scanned the unheated lobby, noting that the lightbulbs were kept dingily low and the whole place smelled of rotgut wine. Harry, behind the reception desk, looked up, saw Sam, and shrunk away from the wood grain counter toward the relative safety of the switchboard behind him. Sam, elbows on the counter, leaned toward him.

"For God's sake, come home. Isn't it better than this flop-house?" he asked. "Don't worry about the family—you can tell them all to go to hell. Just get back there. Francie needs you. Everyone wants you back."

"They don't want me back," Harry countered. "All they care about is what happens to their sister. Everyone wants me back, sure, so she'll be okay. I've had it with that."

Harry was right. They did love him when he was folded into the family. But they didn't want him back on his own. Only for Francie.

At night in his single room occupancy, he must have thought about going back. Even Jen's tufted headboard, how good it would feel to lean his head against it. Then he remembered trudging back to that bed the night Jen had swatted him away. He thought about Minna, how she loved him loved him loved him, sure, but not enough to save him, never mind getting Francie out of Jen's clutches. He thought about how he disgusted himself, those rolls of flab, that weak little nothing between his legs. Sometimes he'd think about how Francie and he had really been made for each other, if only … he turned in bed … waiting to get up in the morning with just enough money to lose it at the card table, and then go to his rotten son-of-a-bitch job, where he could make enough money to lose it again. It was better. Not better. Bearable.

"Harry," Sam asked, "are you in any kind of trouble? Do you owe anyone money?"

Harry cast a rabbity look around the lobby. A few men in

torn armchairs were sleeping it off, no one who could account for his sudden fear.

"We'll loan you the money," Sam said. "Hell, we'll give it to you and no one will ever say one more word about it."

Harry murmured furtively, "Let them kill me, so what. I have no life anyway."

Either Harry had seen too many gangster movies or he came by melodrama naturally.

"But you do have a life," Sam said. "You have a place back in Boston with our family, it's your family, too."

Harry could have dictated his own terms. No more living with Jen. He could have moved back into the family's embrace, warm and stifling, a hero for saving Francie.

"I can't do it, Sam. Leave me alone, pretend I never existed. Tell Francie she's a good kid but I can't help her."

Sam reached over the counter as though to collar Harry. He looked in Harry's eyes, saw the shaking jowls, smelled the fear. Harry wasn't coming back.

AFTERWARD SAM TOOK himself to dinner at Keen's Chop House. Relieved to have dispatched his errand, he ordered a stiff drink, Canadian Club on the rocks. With it he ordered prime rib, medium rare, and then finished off his meal with key lime pie. He needed all the gratification he could get. He was disgusted by Harry, disheartened at his own failure, and not looking forward to the hell he'd have to pay when he got home.

But he wasn't a man to stay down for long. With a pleasantly full stomach, he strolled over to Penn Station enjoying the rush of people around him, entering the vaulted waiting room, and looking up at the schedules posted under the big Benrus clock. He chose a local so he could have a good long sleep and postpone having to deliver the bad news.

Francie was keeping vigil at Minna's, waiting for Sam to phone. When he didn't, Minna was pretty sure the news was bad but she didn't let on.

Sam walked in, wrinkled topcoat over his arm, hat in hand.

"Francie, I'm sorry," he said.

Francie stumbled over a few words. "How was he? What did he say?"

Wearily, Sam told her. "He said no."

Francie hugged her arms around her chest. Harry had failed her. Minna had failed her. Jen had failed her. Sam had failed her. She wept and wept and could not stop. It was the end of her possible years.

II.

AS THEIR MOTHER'S STRENGTH FAILED, MINNA, JEN, AND my mother began to make arrangements to move her into a nursing home. There was no question about Bennie coming with her; she wanted to keep her son beside her always. My friend, the one who'd been admiring of the support my family gave to Bennie, said of my grandmother, "They don't make people like this anymore." One part of me agreed; there was a nobility to her. Another part of me said to myself, Thank God.

As usual Jen stepped in with her money; she gave Bennie's caretaker a generous final payment, enough to return home, where he might have remembered our family as shelter in a storm, or perhaps as a nightmare best forgotten.

Bennie did well at the nursing home. He even made a few friends of a sort, women who saw in him the submissive sons they'd never had, others who were hard of hearing and found it undemanding to sit beside him in the home's dining room.

This new chapter in their lives lasted for three years, a relatively tranquil time. Then my grandmother's breathing became more labored. One day her doctor briskly straightened up from her bedside, stethoscope around his neck, and gestured to my mother and Minna to meet him outside the room. He had heard a crackling sound, a sign that her congestive heart failure was reaching a critical stage. The back of her hospital bed had to be raised a little higher each day until she was sleeping almost sitting up, and even that wasn't helping her to breathe.

The end was near, and then it was nearer, and then she began to let go of her life, of the more than seventy years, the good, the bad, the hard, never the soft; the berry on a branch she'd seen from a cart as she was leaving her shtetl; the howl she had let loose on the world.

Minna was the first to be called. She called Jen and asked her to call Francie. Then she called my mother and asked her to call Pauline.

As she dialed, my mother turned to me. "She'll never get down here in time," she said in the tone that was always there when she spoke of Pauline, anticipating disappointment from the time when Pauline hadn't loved her back with passion to match her own.

But Pauline did get there. All the sisters were at their mother's bedside, women now in their forties and early fifties, still carrying their childhood wounds, still making a circle.

"She knew she was dying," Pauline said. "She spoke to each one of us using a different tone of voice, and she said different things to each of us."

I like to imagine that she looked first to Minna, saying, "Take care of everyone."

Minna sighs inwardly; this had been what was asked of her for as long she could remember.

To Jen, she might have said, "Thank you, my Jennie, for everything you did for me."

Jen stands there, stalwart but hurt, realizing that her mother's gratitude was the most she was ever going to get.

To my mother, she said, "You're a good girl."

My mother pats her mother's hand, hearing those unsatisfying words she'd heard many times before.

"Stay close to your sisters," she said. I see Pauline hearing this and nodding yes, caught up in the moment.

If she could have raised her arm, she might have chucked Francie under the chin. "Smile, *mein kind,* it isn't so bad."

In the last minutes, if she had a thought it would have been of Bennie, who at the very end was brought from his room to hers.

Bennie, expressionless as always, stood by his mother's bed.

"Take care of him," she said of the love of her life, the boy who had been on her mind every waking minute since he'd become ill.

My mother walked him to his room and hurried back.

Swollen feet, swollen ankles, swollen fingers, swollen wrists. Her lips turned blue.

Pauline pulled the blanket up to her mother's chin and tucked it around her shoulders. My mother closed her mother's eyes. Minna bent down and put her cheek against her mother's.

They left, practical women who had to make arrangements, women who had made lives for themselves for better and worse, decent lives, the kind they had set out to make.

They left, children who were bereft.

OUT OF NOWHERE, Pauline began to question Minna, "Where's the red dress? The one Mama brought from Vilna? With the coins in the hem? I had it and I don't know what happened to it. I've been looking everywhere …"

Minna phoned around and tracked down the dress. She reported back to Pauline that she knew where it was, in the closet of a cousin.

But Pauline didn't seem to take in the fact that she was being given an answer. She went on lamenting the loss of the dress.

Minna eventually wangled the dress out of the closet. She phoned Pauline.

"I have the dress."

Pauline acted as though she hadn't heard.

Minna persisted. "I Have The Dress!"

Pauline didn't seem to take it in. It wasn't because she was hard of hearing, or obtuse. Her fidelity to the story, so hard for her to give up, was to a piece of fabric that had once held her mother's body. To find it, only a dress after all, would be to know that it was empty.

Eventually I saw the dress in Pauline's closet, a little red cotton housedress faded by sun and washings. Could *that* be the red dress? I'd pictured crimson silk, the hem stitched in gold thread—a dress made to order for a grandchild who endowed the past with greater splendor than it ever had.

Then I understood. That *was* it, the red dress, neither bright nor fresh as it once had been, not dazzling and sumptuous, but hanging in the closet in the space between a memory and a story.

And the gold coins, provision for a disrupted life?

Gone, as the hem had come undone.

THE QUESTION WAS what to do about Bennie after their mother's death. Then the sisters realized the answer was nothing. He was fine right where he was, staying on at the nursing home.

My mother toted his laundry to our house to wash and iron. My father brought the clothes back starched and neatly folded, smelling of Ivory Snow.

Every month my father went to the nursing home to shave the back of Bennie's neck, a task for which the attendants were too busy. He sat Bennie in a chair and draped a towel around him. Using his own razor that he'd brought from home, my father removed the hairs with careful downward strokes.

Sometimes I kept him company, silently wondering how my father could bring himself to do this intimate service for Bennie who went on being repulsive to me with his flaccid body and fat fingers.

"You can't reach back there," my father said with a wink at me, "unless you want to take a chance of losing your head."

When he was done, Bennie's back hairline was straight, demarcating the salt-and-pepper hair above from the babylike skin below. My father folded the towel and carried it to the wastepaper basket, shaking it out until most of Bennie's hairs had fallen from it.

Bennie hadn't said a word.

Later, I asked my father why he went out of his way for Bennie, who wasn't even his own brother and who didn't seem to care one way or another.

"Look," my father said, "he's a human being, isn't he?"

Oh my sweet father, who knew why shaving the back of a neck is important. It requires the help of another. No one can do it for himself.

I AM SURPRISED now when I realize that Bennie was leading a better life than Rosemary Kennedy, the girl who couldn't keep up with the rest of her boisterous family, who was just a little bit slow, a bit difficult, an embarrassment to her father and, for all her privilege, had come out of the operation permanently disabled, para-lyzed on one side, incontinent and unable to speak coherently. For the remainder of her life she lived with a hired private nurse in a house built especially for her on the grounds of St. Coletta School for Exceptional Children in Wisconsin, while Bennie had gone on living with his mother, supported by Jen, surrounded by his sisters, cared for by Mr. Adams and later by nurses in a good nursing home near the rest of his family. He was taken out to family gatherings, to Pauline's backyard for a cookout.

I showed this photograph to a friend who knew nothing about Bennie and asked him to tell me what he saw in it.

He bent down to the computer screen. "He's detached, but he's okay. His expression is kind of stoic."

He looked again. "The weird thing is the arm that's hanging. It looks inert. The other arm is active—look at the way he's holding the spatula. It's a picture of incongruities. Who is he? A professor?"

Ah … the bow tie! That's why he looks professorial to my friend. I told him about Bennie, how his sisters used to take care that he was dressed nicely when he went out, in a starched white shirt and bow tie.

He subjected the snapshot to closer scrutiny. "The way he's standing there, he seems too perfect, as though someone had posed him that way."

Bennie in the backyard.

When I looked at the photograph again, magnifying it, Bennie is wearing an apron with a word on it: "Barbecute."

When I looked again, I saw a more fundamental strangeness, a person at the farthest reaches of not being at home in the world, in the midst of a tribe that had damaged him and also kept him safe.

12.

ON A WARM DAY IN JUNE, BENNIE STOOD AT AN OPEN window, looking down at a driveway where a little girl was jumping rope. She tripped and dropped the handles. When she bent down to pick up the rope, her braids swung forward.

Bennie turned to Minna. "She changed her hair ribbons," he said. "Yesterday they were blue."

Minna, in as ordinary a tone as she could manage, asked, "Is she someone you know, Bennie?"

"I see her playing in the yard."

With no more fanfare than a child's change of hair ribbon, Bennie had broken his almost fifteen years of silence.

Minna said, "I'll be right back, Bennie." She walked into the residents' dining room to find my mother.

She put her finger to her lips.

"Helen, don't say anything," she whispered, "Bennie is talking."

My mother went back to Bennie's room. He turned around from the window.

"How are you, Bennie?" my mother asked.

"Fine," he said.

IT WAS THE last time Bennie answered with a single word. Once he began to speak, he couldn't stop. The simplest greeting set off an unstoppable cascade of words, as though his brain had been rewired but the electrician had left out the circuit breaker.

"President Truman he's a good man he wore a bow tie did you hear about Frank Sinatra he divorced that wife of his the little girl I could eat her up she's so cute those boys throw stones at me when I come back from the barber's he told me Bess Truman is going to play on the piano a concert no that's her daughter what's her name Margaret that's no name for a Jewish girl she thinks Uncle Miltie is so nice she's going to give him a kiss right on the top of his head ... "

My mother and aunts smiled as though to a child, saying, "That's enough, Bennie." It was never enough. Once started in his monotonous voice, Bennie could be halted only by distracting him, which my mother did by turning to another subject, and Pauline did by bringing sweets. Another way was to ignore him and walk away, which I did.

Bennie had a condition called perseveration, common in cases of frontal lobe damage and sounding quite a bit like the word salad of schizophrenia but fundamentally different. Bennie spoke in an endless chain characterized by "fragments of a previous task attaching themselves to the new one, resulting in strange hybrid designs." To my mother and aunts, Bennie had become a different child but a child nonetheless. To me, he had become an unwitting surrealist. Those magazines whose pages he had silently turned, the radio and television programs that had been turned on in the living room where he had once sat, all of it had been registering in his mind not as memories or stories but as separate bits, one attached to the next by loopy links. As neurologist Elkhonon Goldberg writes, "In my native Russian language, there is an expression *bez tsarya v golovye*, or a head without the czar inside. This expression could have been invented to describe the effects of frontal lobe damage on behavior." My uncle Bennie's czar had decamped, leaving him with a littered field.

ONE DAY WHEN I was in high school and at home with the flu, I received a Get Well note from my Uncle Bennie. A Get Well message from a lobotomized uncle is a very strange thing to receive. At the time I didn't pay much attention, but I must have known it was unusual because I saved it all these years.

A question jumps out as I look at it now: how had Bennie been able to write this? Did my mother dictate it to him? Did Minna? Quite possibly. But neither my mother nor Minna would have thought to write that last line, the one that refers to our annual Thanksgiving dinners at my cousin's house. More likely they would have ended the note on the generic greeting card phrase, "road to recovery."

I can see them standing behind their brother, asking, "Is there anything else, Bennie?"

Yes.

Hope.

But Bennie wasn't supposed to hope. In *Mapping the Mind*, medical writer Rita Carter characterizes the lobes as the place "where ideas are created, plans constructed, thoughts joined with their associations to form new memories and fleeting perceptions held in mind until they are dispatched to long-term memory or oblivion." In other words, Bennie was supposed to have lost pretty much everything that mattered.

But yet he did write "hope."

What could he have meant?

Could Bennie even "mean"?

A Little Primer on the Frontal Lobes

I'VE GLEANED QUITE a lot about them from various sources and have come away with a huge respect for those lobes, as well as a healthy dose of skepticism.

Frontal lobes: most recently evolved and especially human part of the brain ...

Central role: releases the organism from fixed repertoires and reactions, allows the mental representation of alternatives, of imagination, of freedom.

Without the great development of the frontal lobes in the human brain (coupled with the development of the language areas), civilization could never have arisen.

The intentionality of the individual is invested in the frontal lobes, and these are crucial for higher judgment, for imagination, for empathy, for identity, for "soul."

The lobotomized person cannot care. In the idea of caring, there is the essential role of the future, which lobotomy destroys.

[The lobes are] ... what make us specifically human—human beings able to integrate new knowledge, synthesize, plan, innovate, create. A sense of a malleable future, and a coherent self.

When illness strikes at the frontal lobes, what is lost then is no longer an attribute of your mind. It is your mind, your core, your self.

I had said "primer." Perhaps a better word might be "commemoration." I have a feeling that we're living in the age of the frontal lobes, and that soon it will be over. There's a gee whiz quality to all this; "We have found the key and this is it." Every bone in my body says don't believe it, that it will turn out that there is neither key nor location to being human.

13.

IN MY JUNIOR YEAR OF HIGH SCHOOL, I REALIZED MY choices for college were black and white: either I lived at home and commuted, or I had to get a huge scholarship. There were plenty of good colleges in Boston, but I thought I'd die if I had to stay amid the suffocating life of my family. Looking back, I think that wasn't an exaggeration; it would have been the death of my spirit.

I had to get that scholarship. One college required an essay on who I would like to have been; I narrowed my choices down to Eleanor Roosevelt—brilliant, influential, yet restricted by her role and gender—or Aristotle, whose scope had been unlimited but who was perhaps too analytical: did I really want to go through life classifying everything?

Remembering the girl I was, I'm swept by fondness for her as she weighed those choices in all seriousness. In the end I chose Aristotle because his ideas had lasted and that was important to me.

AT THE TIME when college was foremost in my classmates' minds, my father lost his store to the Elm Farms Supermarket, no longer a rumor but a bricks and mortar reality that drained away his customers. He tried working as a counterman in the meat section of a supermarket, but he was used to being his own boss and wasn't cut out for taking orders. After he was fired, he sat for a year in an armchair sunk into what I now think was a serious depression, not bottomless like Francie's but terrible nonetheless. He must have done something other than sitting in that chair, but my memory of this time is so strong that it seems like one long uninterrupted heartbreak. I tried to make him feel better by telling him that my mother and I loved him, and that our love made him a success in life. It didn't work.

I needed his signature on a scholarship application. I brought him a bottle of black ink, a fountain pen, and the form, which I'd already filled out. He got up and looked around for a flat writing surface.

Nearby was a table with a raised drop-leaf. I was pretty sure it wouldn't take any weight, not even handwriting a name. "Please, don't put it there," I pleaded but he didn't pay any attention to me. He started to sign. His hand slipped, the table collapsed, the ink spilled over the application onto the rug. I cried out, "How could you do this to me?" My father fell to his knees and dropped his head into his hands, crying again and again, "I can't do anything right, I can't do anything right."

It was awful. My mother and I were in shock; I see us there, unmoving, my mother with her hand at her mouth, me backing a bit away in horror that my chances were ruined and at the same time wanting to step forward to comfort my father on his knees.

WORTHLESSNESS WAS A familiar if concealed companion in outwardly confident mid-century America, especially so for women. Being without value is a partial explanation for a terrible statistic: twice as many women as men were lobotomized. Of the 241 lobotomies carried out at Stockton State Hospital, 205—or 85 percent—were performed on women.

Wanting to prove that his operation got results, Walter Freeman created a criterion by which to measure its success: whether or not a lobotomized person could return to work. But he built in a double standard. For men, work was defined as engaging in activity outside the home. For women, it was the performance of simple household tasks within the home, which most lobotomized women could do. With this manipulation, Freeman pumped up the numbers of successful lobotomies, claiming his success on the brains of women.

FRANCIE BEGAN TO hear voices. "At night," Minna said, "but they'd go away in the morning."

Minna was concerned that Francie was becoming schizophrenic, but to me noisy visitors who go away in the morning sound a lot like what we all hear in dark times and, if we're lucky, are able to banish in daylight. Again I turned to the psychiatric literature: "A person who becomes depressed can have cognitive symptoms so severe that she has ... delusions ... But these delusions are very different from those of a person with schizophrenia ... in that they are consistent with the person's depressed mood. These kinds of hallucinations apparently do not tell the patient to harm another person. More often the voices badger incessantly, telling the sick person that she is no good, she will always fail, she is worthless."

One woman then in a state mental hospital was Rose Williams. Rose and her younger brother Tom had been the closest of friends when they were children. As one of Tom's biographers has written, "They would race their bikes and cut paper dolls from huge catalogue books, laugh uproariously and invent wonderful new games, her wild imagination a joyous counterpart to his own."

Growing up, Tom had his own version of THE FEELING. Walking home from the movies and going past the church and funeral home across the street, "My heart would ache and I would go into some kind of swoon thinking how mysterious the universe was and how lonely I was in it." He was working all day at the International Shoe Company, then staying up late into the night, writing. He suffered from exhaustion and anxiety attacks about his sexuality. He had to break away, leave home, and travel far away to save himself and become the person he wanted to be, the playwright Tennessee Williams.

Exquisite of feeling in drama, he became numb to the sister he'd left behind, almost as though to respond to Rose's pleas would drag him back to the thwarted life he'd been living. He didn't answer her letters begging him to save her from the hospitals and the shock treatments. It was a year after Rose's lobotomy that he learned it had happened.

Tennessee Williams escaped, abandoned, left hurting Rose knowingly. But he carried Rose with him; when, at the end of *The Glass Menagerie*, Tom, his surrogate, turns in the street, there is Laura (his Rose), standing behind him.

For Rose, as for Francie, abandonment became the breaking point of a fragile mind. There is a clinical condition known as abandonment depression, first identified and described in the writings of James Masterson: "When my patients go through a separation experience that they have been defending themselves against all their lives, the separation brings on a catastrophic set of feelings, which I have called an abandonment depression." Those words evoke Rose, and Francie too, each abandoned by a mother who should have been protecting her. When brother and husband left them, it triggered an avalanche that carried the rocks of old grief.

Rose's lobotomy made her incapable of living outside an institution. For the rest of his life her brother tried to atone, treating Rose with exquisite care as though she were the fine crystal treasured by the character Laura in his play.

For Rose it was all too late; she had already broken.

"I THINK WHAT really finished Francie," Minna said, "was the shock treatments. The doctors believed in them so much that Francie was like a guinea pig. She pleaded with the doctors to stop."

I didn't say what I was thinking: "Why didn't you make them stop?" Perhaps she didn't believe that the doctors would listen to her, and maybe, too, she shared their hope that maybe the next one—or the next one after that—would be the one that would make the difference.

I've learned that it was Abraham Myerson, our old family friend, who introduced electric shock therapy to America. Until then I'd been unequivocally proud of my family's association with this man of high intellect and achievement. Myerson's championing of Bennie's lobotomy didn't affect my view of him; I think there had been nothing else to do for Bennie, other than consign him to the horrors of the insane asylum.

But when I read his words on how best to effect a cure through electric shock, I was appalled: "The reduction of intelligence is an important factor in the curative process ... The fact is that some of the very best cures that one gets are in those individuals whom one reduces almost to amentia [feeble-mindedness]."

What sort of a man could urge that doctors should intentionally make their patients feeble-minded?

The best I can come up with is a man who believed he was doing the right thing. That's the heart of it: they all convinced themselves they were doing the right thing—Moniz on women he stole from the asylum; Freeman lobotomizing twenty inmates a day. Otherwise they couldn't have done what they did.

The urge to help can harden into a general principle, at which point almost anything becomes justified. There is little room left for an individual, certainly not for one who may be pleading to stop, as Francie was pleading.

I've come to believe that there was and is a flaw running through medical culture, made even deeper by a larger culture that deems some people lesser. It is the failure to feel what another person is feeling. While this may sound like a failure of empathy (and it is), I mean something beyond that. Empathy has a biological basis; we arrive equipped for it with a passel of mirror neurons that may give us a predisposition for it.

But fellow feeling—a link with another person, a baseline recognition that all of us are in this together, as well as a particularized recognition of the situation of another—that doesn't come with the territory. A person must will it and act upon it; it is a choice.

A STRANGER TELEPHONED Minna. He had found her phone number in Francie's pocket. Francie had been lying half-conscious on the streetcar tracks.

Was she trying to kill herself or had she collapsed from the medications she was taking? No one knew, but it was clear that Francie was in terrible danger.

FRANCIE'S DOCTORS TOLD the family that her case was hopeless. They had tried electric shock and pills; there was nothing else to do, except what they now recommended: a lobotomy. They added, "It won't be like her brother's. We can target the brain now with much more precision. Francie's will be what we call a minimal lobotomy. She'll be able to live alone, shop for herself, manage the basics of her life. Without it, they said, "she'll weep for the rest of her life."

Francie had joined a chorus of weeping women; La Llorona wandering the earth searching for her children; Niobe, turned to stone, her tears falling like a waterfall down the face of the rock. Sorrows chronicled in ancient times trickled down and landed on our exhausted family.

The doctors said that a lobotomy was a last resort for Francie. I used to think of a last resort in terms of a scenario: a person standing at the edge of a cliff about to jump, a compassionate hand extended in rescue. But in the same way that "hopeless" derives its authority by sounding like a diagnosis, "last resort" has its own questionable justification built into it. It is buttressed by a common belief in the twentieth and twenty-first centuries, at least in the developed world, that there has to be something we can do to make things better. We have the means; we can always move on to another advance, another technology that promises a solution. In this scenario, which asserts that any means should be tried, the person on the cliff is not an individual but rather the representative of a challenge to find that next thing.

"We come to them who weep foolishly, and sit down and cry for company, instead of imparting to them truth and health in rough electric shocks, putting them once more in communication with their own reason." In Emerson's words, I hear a cultural briefing to usher in extreme treatments for the mentally ill. Reason valued over emotion; bracing "reality" over compassion; the general good over the worth of the individual whose weeping, like Francie's, may not be foolish at all.

FRANCIE PHONED HER sisters all the time, one after another, her anguish cycling through their days and nights.

In the darkness, they had thoughts they couldn't admit in daylight.

I can't stand her.

I'm getting sick myself.

Sometimes I think it would be better if she did kill herself.

It would end her suffering.

Sometimes I think it would be better for us.

I'm so ashamed. I can't tell anyone I think this.

THEY GATHERED AT Minna's, my uncles zipped into their winter corduroy car coats, my aunts with hats pulled low over their ears. Their cheeks when they kissed one another were like ice.

Jen came in from Central Square with a shopping bag from her store. She handed the bag to Minna, who understood she was to give it to Francie, who wouldn't look at the clothes inside.

Pauline and her husband had driven down from the North Shore, feeling a little self-satisfied at having sacrificed other obligations but understanding this was an emergency.

Nearby on a wall hung the 1915 family photograph as it did on the walls of the other sisters, the picture that did not include Francie as even now the meeting was going on without her. All of them felt the pathos of Francie's situation, but they were acutely aware it wasn't fair. Here they were again, having to debate the same awful choice, not knowing what to do. But they were very different people than when they'd conferred about Bennie's lobotomy, no longer young women, not united by timidity.

Minna began the family council by saying, "She doesn't want it."

My father took a slice of Minna's sour cream coffee cake.

"This is good, Minna," he said. "I don't blame her, look what happened to Bennie."

Minna qualified. "It won't be like that, like Bennie's. The doctors say it's something new they call minimal."

Pauline, her skepticism aroused toward anything she saw as possibly falling under Minna's control, asked, "How do we know?"

When she spoke she sounded testy and aggrieved, as though her sisters had purposely kept information from her.

My mother said, "You have to trust somebody."

They took a break while Minna phoned Francie, the nightly checking-in call that I remember my mother making as well.

"The same." Minna returned with a report. "She has a terrible migraine, she's crying."

Pauline said, "What else did you expect?"

Sam spoke loudly, startling them back into debate. "She wants to keep you jumping at her beck and call."

"Sam!" Minna chastised her husband, "That's not nice."

"Nice, nice! She manipulates you. That's how she gets her hooks into you. I could use a stiff drink. What about you, Jen?"

Jen, the only one of the sisters who enjoyed a drink, liked Cuba Libres.

"Not tonight, Sam, I have to be at the store early."

Jen looked tired. She was working harder than ever, and her smoking wasn't doing her any good.

Sam went over to the sideboard and bent down stiffly—his knees had been giving him trouble—and got out the bottle of Canadian Club. He poured himself a shot.

My father reached for another slice of the coffee cake, but before he could get to it my mother pushed the plate farther away.

Sam laid out the options. "Number one: She could stay in the hospital. We know what will happen there, they'll keep giving her shock treatments. It won't help. Number two: We can take her out of the hospital, but then where—?"

Jen interrupted, "Her room is waiting, she doesn't have to do anything, she can have anything she wants—"

Pauline, remembering what had happened when Francie had lived with Jen before, balked at Jen's self-deception: "Oh yes ... and try to kill herself."

Jen sat silent and wounded.

"What if we don't do anything?" Pauline threw in the wild card.

Jen was appalled. "Leave her to rot?"

Minna wanted to keep the peace: "I'm sure that's not what Pauline meant."

Pauline could stand up to Jen. "Don't put words in my mouth. I mean give her time. We're all so taken up with her problems. It may not be doing her any good."

"By the way Pauline," Sam retorted, "where are we supposed to put her, while we 'give her time?'"

Pauline and Sam had been skirmishing for years. She claimed he'd never believed her when her son Phil was sick, their animosity further aroused by a recent spat. Sam had got a good deal on a cemetery plot, but it depended on everyone in the family agreeing to it. Pauline had refused. Sam had given her a hard time, saying "Are you better than everyone else?" She had said, "Don't bury me in a lump."

Pauline's husband, a quiet and mild man, asked, "Would a change of scene help, maybe if Jen took her away again on a trip—like Cuba, you remember Jen?"

"She's not strong enough," Minna replied. "All those shock treatments weakened her system."

There was no argument to this: they all knew that Francie's health had been compromised.

"How about a Hoodsie, anyone?" Minna asked.

Minna went into the kitchen and came back with paper cups of ice cream, half vanilla, half chocolate. She always had a supply; she ate a Hoodsie every night.

"If she doesn't want to have the operation," Jen put in, "we can't make her ... "

"You should talk, Jen." Pauline flared. "She didn't want to live with you, but you made her. And look what happened."

My mother said, "What's done is done," the same words she'd said before when, according to Pauline, she'd rebuffed her sister's attempt to reestablish their friendship, the words a statement of what she saw as fact, putting a period to the end of possibility.

Jen looked over to Minna for reassurance.

Again Minna tried to calm the waters. "Everyone meant well."

It was understood by all that Minna had power of attorney but that she wouldn't want to use it.

Sam said, "Can you get me a real spoon, Minna? These little wooden things are useless. Look, let's face it. She won't be the same. We can't kid ourselves. But it's not like she's going to be all right, ever."

Pauline shot out, "How do you know? What makes you so sure?"

My mother asked, "What exactly did the doctors say about what will happen to her if she has the lobotomy and if she doesn't?"

Minna responded, "They say she'll forget the bad things. They say she won't suffer."

Pauline's husband dropped his moderate tone and blurted out, "It's a barbaric operation. Should people be turned into zombies so they can 'feel better'?"

"Feel nothing," Pauline said, backing him up.

Minna said, "You haven't seen how bad things are. Where have you been all this time?"

"I was there when Bennie was growing up. I remember him as he was. His lobotomy was a travesty, but no one listened to me and you won't now."

"No, Pauline, you remember Bennie as you want to, you stop your memories where it's convenient."

"He taught me to play kick the ball."

"I wasn't out playing," Minna retorted. "It was all I could do to help Mama take Bennie back and forth and stop her hysterics."

"I wouldn't give in to her," Pauline said. "I'd do something that would make her smile."

"You were the little princess."

There was a pause as everyone heard the children they'd once been.

My mother went on, "Look at some of the people we know, like Mrs. Goldfarb in Coolidge Corner. She still has nightmares about Auschwitz. Maybe she'd do anything to forget the camps."

"The operation has to do some good," Jen put her oar back in. "Otherwise that doctor wouldn't have got the prize."

"You don't think that just happened, do you?" my father said. "I bet it was fixed."

"Fixed—are you crazy?" Sam raised his voice. "Nobody fixes the Nobel Prize."

"Okay, have it your way. I know what I know." My father went around to the other side of the dining room table, evading my mother's reach. He cut himself a slice of cake.

Sam said, "Let's vote, yes or no, on a piece of paper."

"For God's sake, Sam." Jen said. "We can't settle things that way."

It was the old unbowed Jen, countering Sam with the knowledge that Francie's fate could hinge on his suggestion.

"How else, Jen?" Sam asked. "Does anyone have any other ideas?"

Pauline replied, "Wait. Give her time. She isn't even forty yet, she still has her life in front of her. Maybe she'll get better."

Pauline and her husband looked around at everyone else.

My mother said sadly, "That's a fantasy, Pauline."

They decided that they weren't getting anywhere. Buttoning their coats, they knew something had to be done. They'd come back to it later.

MINNA WANTS TO mull over what they should do about Francie, what she herself should do, but tonight after the family meeting she is very tired. She sits in the center of her living room couch. It is the middle of the night and her quilted light blue robe is zipped up the center to keep out the chill. Sam is asleep in the next room.

The couch has become her habitat ever since Sam took over the easy chair, and who can blame him; it's more comfortable for him ever since his colostomy. While he has been scrupulous about taking care of himself, their apartment has an ever-present slight smell of room spray and trouble.

They both are getting older. Minna's back aches in a way it never did when she was still in her forties, which wasn't even all that long ago. Most of the time she accepts that this is what it is, aging. Tonight it feels unfair, one more thing.

Everyone tells Minna that she is too thin, and it is true, she is like a board, never had breasts, never for that matter really had a body. Tonight she has a body, a well-fed one, as it happens, even though she never puts on weight. They all stay thin, her sisters, too. She knows that for other people it can feel like an insult against appetite, the ordinary kind that overwhelms, that is about nothing but need and comfort, the whole chicken, skin and all, eaten at one go. No, these are the women of one slice, no, no more, that's enough.

Minna's Hoodsie is on the coffee table untouched, as is her book *Memoirs of Harry Truman: Year of Decisions*. She has been reading about the founding of the United Nations, an organization of which she deeply approves, its methods of conciliation attuned to her own personality. But tonight her bookmark remains in place.

Everyone is asleep. Not only Sam. Francie and Helen and Jen and Pauline—they are all asleep. Minna knows this as surely as when they were all children together when she, the watchdog, lay awake listening for their breathing.

From across the hall, she hears a cousin by marriage fumbling with his key. A widower, he lives alone and Minna feels sorry for him. Often she'll open the door to ask whether he'd like a piece of coffee cake. But not tonight.

Tonight Minna is a horse coming up to the hurdle and shying away. She is hearing Francie's whiny voice, and her weeping, that endless weeping, and before Minna is overwhelmed by pity—her virtually automatic response—she is choked with rage and revulsion.

Maybe it's because she's so tired. Maybe it's because she has been vigilant for so long. If only she could get into her own bed, twin size would be fine, away from Sam ... if only she could wake up and Francie would not be there, always phoning first thing in the morning.

Can't Francie get hold of herself?

She feels something rising in her body, an urge to slap Francie. Instantly, she is shocked at herself. When did the well of pity—endless, or so she had thought—run dry?

Minna knows she will never beat her fists against a windowsill. She will never have an affair with a married man. She will never move away or lose herself in sex. She knows who she is, and what she will always be. The eldest. The one who has borne the burdens. The one who goes on.

A Hoodsie is a little thing, four ounces, maybe, of ice cream. If there were a pint of ice cream in the refrigerator, tonight Minna would eat it all. Sam snores, reminding her of the room beyond this one. He needs her. They all need her.

She turns off the three-way bulb, dim to regular to bright, a full round before it goes dark. She bends back the little cardboard tab on the ice cream lid, takes a few mouthfuls, her spoon dipping back in with the habit of years.

BACK IN HER own home, Pauline would like to call her best friend and complain about her sisters. But that's not her way; she thinks it would diminish her in her friend's eyes, although she has been heard to say that this friend is more of a sister than her own sisters, and knows that her friend accepts her for who she is. As always though she's concerned about how she appears in the eyes of another, and something more: she has an idea of nobility that she would like to rise to. This has always been her strength: aspiration for a better way to live, a better way to be, evident in her appetite for learning. Her formal education didn't go beyond high school, but for many years she has been taking courses at Harvard's Lifelong Learning Center, where she has no hesitation about writing papers in which she hauls Samuel Johnson onto the carpet for his treatment of his friend Mrs. Thrale. It was, Pauline wrote, as though their friendship had never existed, an unwitting echo of my mother's and her own long time grievances against each other.

She has reserved her greatest passion for Emily Dickinson and fiercest anger at Dickinson's friend Thomas Wentworth Higginson, taking him to task for his suppression of Dickinson's publishing hopes. Pauline feels that she knows too well what it is to be suppressed.

She calls her best friend after all, complaining about her sisters' ignorance, their motives. She talks about their disapproval when she took her father in for the last years of his life. She had sought him out, thinking he might need a place to come in from the cold, and yes, she had needed him, a parent of her own.

She says, "They thought I was giving shelter to the enemy. But he wasn't the bad person my sisters made him out to be."

Then, not realizing how similar she is to her sisters—their helpfulness and their illusions—she adds, "I fixed up our guest room so that it was nice for him, all in blue with a blue bedspread and blue curtains. He was happy to be there."

WHILE HER SISTERS and brothers-in-law have been trying to come to a decision about her fate, Francie too has been thinking.

It is nighttime and she is wide awake.

She is sitting at the edge of her narrow hospital bed.

Across from her is Bennie, who comes to her now at night, an apparition in that big chair from their mother's house.

She looks at him silently, at the face without expression that haunts her.

She is seeing what she may become.

Knowing he can never answer, she cannot ask: "My brother, what should I do?"

14.

WHEN FRANCIE CAME BACK FROM THE HOSPITAL AFTER her lobotomy, her features seemed to be the same as they'd been before. But they weren't. Her face was pulled forward as if it had come back from the hospital a size smaller. Her shoulders were hunched, her head down, her speech a monotone.

It was true, what the doctors had predicted. She didn't weep endlessly. She was able to live by herself in her own studio apartment, do a little shopping, visit us if someone drove her. The doctors said Francie was one of the fortunate ones for whom the operation had worked.

Had it? One night Francie phoned my mother to tell her with pride that she'd made a TV dinner all by herself. My mother understood that for Francie—Francie, as she was now—this was a genuine feat, while inside she mourned her sister who had once so delicately tapped and released the bombe.

When people weren't looking, Francie would rifle through purses and cabinets, searching for an errant pill. As soon as she felt herself unwatched she would disappear into the bathroom.

"Where is she?" my mother would ask the first few times this happened, speaking aloud to herself. Then she'd hear the sound of running water.

My mother stood at the bathroom door.

"Are you all right, Francie?" she called out. "Say something." The door was locked.

"Come out of there," my mother said in a louder voice, jiggling the doorknob.

The sound of a toilet flushing.

Francie had been gulping down whatever medications she could find, then destroying the evidence. Tracks covered, she emerged, head turned away from my mother, her expression furtive and sly. No one knew whether she had developed an addiction or whether she was still trying to kill herself or whether she was trying to feel something—anything—that would let her know she was alive.

Francie was included in everything the family did, a cookout at Norumbega Park, a wedding, a bar mitzvah, an evening out at the Latin Quarter nightclub. In photos of family gatherings, Francie usually sits next to Bennie, the two of them side by side.

Francie and Bennie

AIIIEEE! A DREAM—A woman with a gauze bandage wrapped around her head like a tennis headband. She is sporty, suburban, chatting away with a salesclerk, seeming perfectly normal, happy to have had a lobotomy. I want to scream and scream, "No—don't do it, it's not good!"

What was wrong with my family?

Bennie was one thing.

But Francie? After they had seen what happened to Bennie? After she said she didn't want the lobotomy?

Think about it—I have said this to myself for years—really think about it—

waking your sister—

taking her to the hospital—

handing her over—

to an operation that you know will at least partially erase her.

It's still unbearable.

"It was the times," Minna has said.

Yes, that's a widely offered explanation. But it doesn't hold up. Yes, things were accepted then that wouldn't be accepted now.

But that's true for each and every time.

They must have thought they were doing the right thing. All of them.

Jen, bulldozing Francie. Minna, refusing to rescue Francie.

What was wrong with them?

I ONCE ASKED Dan whether he thought our mothers and aunts had saved themselves at Francie's expense.

He thought about it for a few seconds and said, "Yes. But you know it really was her or them."

What would I have done?

I would have rented a small cottage near a peaceful beach and taken Francie there. It would be a distance away from other people but close enough to walk and buy groceries. I would bring a lot of books and magazines and be very quiet. If Francie wept all the time and I couldn't stand it (which I couldn't), I'd say, "Weep all you want, but I have to ask you to do it in your own room."

I see Francie venturing out of her room at night, alone under a porch light, leafing through magazines. I see us cooking together, a light meal with a minimum of fuss. We'd stay as long as she needed. Toward the end we might go to a movie or two. And then we'd come back. But not to the family. Francie might come back to a self she'd never really known but that was out there waiting for her.

Francie

In my mind I hear my mother saying, That's a fantasy, Janet.

I hear myself saying back to my mother, It may be a fantasy but at least it's something that might have helped her. That's better than what you did. You were supposed to love Francie.

Is this what love is?

15.

I HEARD ABOUT FRANCIE'S POST-LOBOTOMY LIFE FROM the distance of college.

I had managed it; I had got away. An adventurous young professor brought Antonioni's film *L'Avventura* to campus. Overwhelmed at its end, walking across that grassy playing field, I felt myself tilt with the earth's axis. Back in my room, I sat on an Indian print bedspread, listening to John Coltrane. I was tickled by Gregory Corso's poem "Marriage," infused with his knowledge that if he didn't follow the conventional path he'd end up alone in a furnished room, pee stains on his underwear. He pictured himself trying to be an ordinary husband—really trying, but failing in spite of himself—ending up in desperation leaving notes for the milkman: "Penguin dust, bring me penguin dust." Increasingly I knew that my life would be spent with others of my kind, that it would be a life of penguin dust.

One evening during my sophomore year, during my weekly phone call home, my mother told me that my father's second attempt at a store had failed. He'd chosen the wrong location and gone bankrupt. As my mother spoke, I pictured my affable father when his first store was doing well, standing beside a gleaming case displaying lamb chops, fresh and pink, curling around each other. I saw him coming up the stairs carrying big paper bags, cornucopias of food he brought home every night from the store. I saw his seven-day-a-week ox-life, carrying haunches of meat up from the basement. Then I saw him waiting in the store, day after day, for customers who had deserted him and customers who had never come.

I looked around at the other students in my dorm and hated them with the black and white ferocity of an eighteen-year-old. They were girls who took privilege for granted, who could never understand my life shot through with lobotomized relatives, and fathers who had failed.

I closed myself in a stall in the ladies room—a regular retreat for months afterward—and tried to soothe myself by eating chocolate bars behind a locked door. We were not good enough. I was not good enough.

The family disease had caught up with me.

I BEGAN TO skip classes, taking a train to New York at a moment's notice, walking alone for hours through safe and unsafe neighborhoods. I have a distinct memory of never wearing socks, even on the coldest of days; a way to say I don't give a damn.

When I had a paper to write, I put it off, nervous bravado assuring me I could pull it off at the last minute as I'd done before. Then one day I couldn't. I sat paralyzed at the typewriter. During the long night that followed, it seemed to me as though everything that mattered, from my scholarship to my right to be alive, depended on writing that paper. But I couldn't do it.

In the morning I went to the library, where I looked in the stacks for books on my subject. I found an old one with yellowing paper and ornate typeface. I looked around. I was alone. I tucked the book under the waistband of my skirt, buttoned my coat around it, and walked out into the cool air. Back in the dorm, I copied the chapter word for word, handing it in that afternoon as my own.

I was caught, of course. I hadn't been a very expert plagiarist: the fusty style gave me away, and I hadn't even altered a sentence or sprinkled the text with some ideas of my own. It had been so straightforward an act of plagiarism that it should have signaled Help.

I was called in, first by my professor. I tried to bluff. The professor accused me of plagiarizing everything I'd published in the college newspaper. Writing now, I can feel terror rising and rage. He gave me no quarter, disdainful toward me and what I'd done, which now seemed one and the same thing. I was certain he'd given up on me forever. I went to a psychiatrist in town, a woman recommended by a kind dean, who seemed a nice enough lady but let me run rings around her, a cool defense that didn't betray what I was feeling.

Suspension—that's a foolish idea—I'm supposed to leave for three months and that's going to make me a better person? And then I get to come back as if nothing happened. I had not caught on to the idea of penance or of forgiveness. Nor did I tell her my deep fear: if I were to take a suspension everyone would know what I had done. No one would want me back.

I walked aimlessly; that year's hit song poured out from radios on the windowsills of dorms: "Moon river, wider than a mile ... Oh, dream maker, you heart breaker ... "

That same kind dean called me into her office, wanting me to understand what I would be giving up if I were to drop out: a scholarship, a fine education, professors who thought I had exceptional promise.

I said to myself, Please don't make me write. I'm bad.

I packed my bags and left.

I WAS BACK home, where Bennie and Francie sat like zombies, where my father stayed up late counting the tips he'd made driving a cab, where I was one of the sick and failed ones.

I went to a psychiatrist—perhaps it was at my mother's suggestion, that time is hazy. I sat in the office of Abraham Myerson's son, also a psychiatrist, thinking that he could never understand me. I didn't tell him about what I'd done; I had to be careful not to reveal too much. He knew my relatives, what they did to its sick members.

That was the spring of shoplifting. I had bad taste; I stole a rabbit vest right after an appointment with Doctor Myerson. After a few episodes, growing progressively bolder, I was caught. I talked my way out of it, which one could do in those days with a display of contrition. Increasingly I thought of myself as a criminal, enjoying my sense of being an outlaw but fearful of what I might do next.

On the spur of the moment, one night a friend and I took a midnight flight to New York without telling anyone where we were going. We went down to Bleecker Street and up to Columbia; we waded in the Steuben fountain across from the Plaza (we had seen Fellini's *La Dolce Vita*); at sunrise we walked through Central Park, where an actor was pacing under a bridge, taking advantage of the good acoustics to recite Dylan Thomas's "Fern Hill." We were protected by the God who sometimes takes care of foolish but adventurous girls, who whispered in my ear, "This is the place for you."

I went back to Boston and waitressed in an already legendary coffee house on Mount Auburn Street, where Tom Rush and the Jim Kweskin Jug Band performed, the often-stoned Fritz Richmond on the washtub bass. I did a number of wild and interesting things, all of which are sufficiently familiar to readers of sixties memoirs that they do not need to be repeated here, except for one all-important experience: I discovered a theater that showed nothing but foreign films—*Seven Samurai, The Passion of Joan of Arc*—and found again the exaltation I thought I'd lost.

That September I got on a bus and went to New York with an inchoate aim of working in film. New York turned out to be the right place for me, as it has always been for people who aren't happy elsewhere. My life began to be what I wanted it to be—rich, complicated, sometimes ecstatic, sometimes depressed, sometimes risky, never boring.

As I had years ago when I made my escape after Thanksgiving dinners, I took long walks, all the while rejoicing in my new city. During the days I worked at odd jobs, mostly in bookstores. At night I studied philosophy in classes taught by melancholic refugees from Germany. I took a class on physics and poetry, wept at Kurt Weill's *Johnny Johnson* and was enchanted by Picasso's *Family of Saltimbanques*. I was a girl of my times. A professor invited me to a party at an apartment house on the Upper West Side famous for its European-style courtyard and the writers who lived there. As I walked into the apartment I was greeted by an aroma I had never smelled before: warm oranges mixing with creamy veined cheeses, a Europe I hadn't yet seen laid out on the buffet table alongside the dark chocolate of the New World. I felt that all of it was for me, the tragic histories and heroic survivals, the ancient cosmologies and the enlightenment rationality, the sensuous delights and heedless excess, a buffet of possibilities I was ready to receive.

I didn't think about my aunt and uncle's lobotomies, never mind mention them to anyone. I dutifully phoned my parents once a week, although in retrospect I was hardly reassuring—I got a kind of sadistic kick out of hinting at my exploits.

Nothing that they told me about the family ever touched me, no dispatches from that other life that had been expected of me. I was reading Heraclitus then and learning that one could never step in the same stream twice. I splashed on—to adventure, love, making films—leaving Bennie and Francie standing in a stagnant pool.

Sometimes as dusk fell in New York I'd find myself on Forty-second Street across from the Public Library or walking down West Twelfth Street and there suddenly would be THE FEELING, that clutch at my heart. A clutch of sadness. A clutch of beauty, people at the curb, crossing the street when the light changed.

BUT I NEVER told anyone about the plagiarism.

Not one word.

I didn't tell my roommates in my first New York apartment on West Seventy-second Street and Riverside Drive.

I didn't tell when I moved downtown.

I didn't tell people at my new job, where I wore nylons every day.

I didn't tell my brilliant professor, not even when we became good friends and, briefly, lovers.

I didn't tell the gorgeous crazy man I made love with in his filthy Avenue A bedroom.

I didn't tell my classmates. I never took writing classes because I didn't trust myself.

I didn't tell when I began to write again, unable finally to stop but worried I was using someone else's words, even though they were my own.

I didn't tell when I published my first book.

I didn't tell my then-husband.

I didn't tell during the divorce when I sat in a cold room and called, "Oh God!"

Not when I learned I had cancer.

Not Bobbi. Not Peggy. Not Melinda. Not my parents. Not Minna, who I think would have forgiven me.

Not when I met the man who is my lifelong husband. Not afterward when we moved to California.

I didn't tell when I published my second book. Or the ones afterward.

I never told a soul.

16.

ON AN ORDINARY DAY IN 1967, BENNIE WALKED IN HIS slow trance-like way toward the dining room of the nursing home. He twirled, not stopping until an attendant came along and turned him toward lunch. He sat down at a round table with other residents. He was silent, his once endless jumble of words slowing like a fan after the current has been turned off.

A bowl of peanuts, shelled and roasted, was on the table, put there at each meal for people who liked to nibble. Eating these peanuts was an unfailing part of Bennie's routine. He put the usual handful into his mouth and tried to swallow. But one peanut refused to go down. It lodged itself, dense, salty, a little pointy at the ends, blocking his windpipe.

There had to have been a moment when Bennie knew panic, when he glimpsed an attendant running toward him with a glass of water, when he felt hearty slaps and timid pats on his back.

But it had to have been over quickly.

My Uncle Bennie was fifty-nine years old when he died choking on a peanut.

I am embarrassed to say that when I heard about it, it struck me as Theater of the Absurd. Later I remembered those Thanksgivings when he would stuff himself with handfuls of dessert and an aunt would say, "It won't go down that way." I read that years after a lobotomy, muscles could still lose their will to swallow.

I debated with myself: Was Bennie's death an accident that could happen to any one of us? Or had it been part and parcel of what had been done to him? I came to the conclusion that Bennie's situation was an extreme version of the unanswerable questions that are posed by everybody's deaths.

He was laid to rest in a grave next to his mother in Sharon Cemetery, where all my maternal relatives are buried. There are no gravestones to break the rolling expanse of small knolls and shade trees; only plaques flush with the grass on which my family's names are inscribed.

AFTER THE FUNERAL, Dan unearthed a photograph that he has emailed me. I opened the *attachment* (oh the language we take for granted), and this is what appears on my screen:

Pauline, Minna, Bennie, Jen, Helen

Bennie is in the midst of what looks like a stage but is probably a family wedding, his sisters surrounding him, propping him up, holding him hostage, keeping him in the center.

Francie is not in this picture, as she was not in the 1915 photo. At this point I think that she no longer wanted, or perhaps was no longer able, to come to the cookouts, the weddings and bar mitzvahs. She too had been surrounded and held hostage.

Is this what love is?—that was the question I'd asked when I imagined myself saving Francie.

I have to answer Yes, this is love. And where did I get the idea that love is only and unequivocally good?

THE SAME YEAR that Bennie died, Walter Freeman performed his third and final lobotomy on Helen Mortensen, one of his first transorbital patients. When it had seemed to her that the effects of each of her earlier lobotomies was wearing off, she requested further surgeries. I cannot understand this—lobotomies don't have expiration dates. But perhaps Mortensen lived in a fight-or-flight state when every lapse—a day's rage, a sighting that might or might not be hallucinatory—seemed to carry a threat to her sanity. In the midst of the third operation Freeman tore a blood vessel in Mortensen's brain. She hemorrhaged and died.

After Freeman's surgical privileges were taken away, he transferred his files into his van and took off alone, driving to Florida, where he underwent surgery for cancer. Recuperating, he learned that one of his sons, thirty-two-year-old Randy, had died from a metastatic brain tumor. Freeman did not return home. He drove through the South, into Ohio, then east to New Jersey, Washington, DC, New York, Boston, and up to Toronto. After thirty years of taking Nembutal every night, he couldn't sleep. He drove on, looking up patients and their relatives in West Virginia, Ohio, Michigan, North Dakota, Idaho, Oregon, and California. Some of the relatives were pleased to see him; others were not.

Sometimes the operation had produced people who could correspond with him, bringing him news of their progress, letting him advise them. He stayed up late writing letters to former patients: "Dear Judy, I was delighted to receive the note from you with its quotation from one of the famous hymns. I suspect that it was by Charles Wesley, the brother of the preacher, the great hymnologist of the 18th century. Maybe, someday … you will sing it for me, with piano accompaniment."

In 1969, Freeman was invited to Mexico. He brushed up on his Spanish and took off on a six-month trip of 22,000 miles. He drove too fast; his eyesight was failing; there were accidents. A year later he wasn't invited to an international conference on psychosurgery in Copenhagen; he went anyway, even though a month before he'd suffered a concussion from a fall on a backpacking trip.

He gave a lecture that focused solely on his own role in the development of psychosurgery. It was met with silence.

In 1972, after several agonizing recurrences of cancer, he drifted into a coma and died.

I am truly surprised at how saddened I am by the end of Freeman's life. I'm not going to be his defender, but his loyalty to his convictions was fierce, and his pain—physical, emotional, human—had to have been unspeakable.

WALTER FREEMAN LEFT behind questions. They are questions of the twentieth century, when they were first raised on a mass scale.

When a person has undergone vast trauma and been left with intolerable anguish, is there a saving grace in the loss of one's self? Would a life without feeling be preferable to one spent in torment?

When I began this investigation, I assumed that lobotomies produced only zombie-like people. But I've learned since that they sometimes provided genuine relief to people who, to my surprise, were able to be aware of their situations, even to compare them with the past and say how much better they were. One trade-off, though, remained constant: the lobotomized remained indifferent. I don't want to put forth a simple-minded embrace of feeling for its own sake; if I were feeling the horrors that Bennie experienced, maybe I'd want to become indifferent, too. Indifference, however, has become a way of life; as we become less and less capable of feeling the pain of others, we come closer to dehumanizing other people, and ourselves as well.

Lobotomy is seen now as a discredited operation, at best an unfortunate precursor to newer and far more precise incursions into the brain. But it also points the way to a twenty-first-century question: In a culture that supports indifference, how can we sustain fellow feeling?

We know our icons of terror: in the twentieth century, the bomb, the iron lung, lobotomy. In the twenty-first century, terrorism, extinction. But I believe that the possibility of dehumanizing people is always with us, at least as great a terror.

1973

FOR ALMOST TWENTY years nothing had been heard from Harry. Francie never asked about him. For that matter, she'd never said a word about her lobotomy. Her capacity to care had been thinned out.

She was in her fifties when she was diagnosed with terminal liver cancer. On the way to visit her, Minna caught sight of Harry's mother in the hospital lobby. She ducked into the gift shop, but Mrs. Gurstein had already spotted her and followed her in. She wanted Minna to know that Harry had come back to Boston and was living with her. Unspoken but understood was the end of her sentence, " ... and not with your family."

She asked about poor Francie, how is she?

Minna, unwilling to volunteer information to the enemy, told her only that Francie was in the hospital. Mrs. Gurstein said that Harry was there, too, and asked what floor Francie was on. Minna offered a number. Mrs. Gurstein said that Harry's room was near Francie's.

Minna nodded politely.

My mother and Minna met up at the hospital cafeteria. Together they argued about whether Francie should be told about Harry, that he was there in the hospital, one floor below her.

"This is a dying woman," my mother said. "She should be able to decide her last wishes."

"No," Minna said. "She's dying. Why should she have more pain?"

"Francie must be told. We owe her that respect." My mother had reached a point in her life when she was no longer diffident. "She is not a child. If you don't tell her, I will."

My mother approached the bed where Francie lay dulled by painkillers and by her lobotomy. Francie looked up as my mother pulled up a chair to the bedside.

"Francie," my mother began, "I want to tell you something. It's about Harry. If you don't want to hear it, say so."

Francie said nothing.

"He's sick, too, not like you are, it's that old phlebitis he used to get."

My mother stopped to give Francie a chance to object. Still she said nothing.

"He's back in Boston. He's here, in the hospital, on the fifth floor."

Francie lay her head back on the pillow and reached over for a swab. She dipped it in ice water and ran it over her chapped lips. Then she asked for a comb to fix her hair.

She asked to be wheeled down to Harry's room.

Down a corridor, past volunteers in pink smocks, nurses padding by in white shoes, making a sharp turn at the nurses' station, my mother wheeled Francie toward Harry.

They peered at the numbers until they found Harry's room. My mother parked the wheelchair, adjusted the brake, and cautiously opened the door.

Harry's eyes were closed. Beside his bed was a walker. Francie stayed in the doorway looking at him, at this sleeping jowly man she had married. She gestured that she didn't want to go any closer.

She didn't say a word. My mother coughed.

Harry opened his eyes, looked up, saw a blur of women, then recognized them as Helen and Minna. Casting his glance downward to the woman who was sitting in the wheelchair, he saw that it was Francie, smaller, withered, the woman he had married.

They looked at each other for a minute. Harry tried for a little smile.

Francie made a small dip of her head.

"That's it, Harry," she said.

She asked to be wheeled back to her room.

A FEW MONTHS later, she died. At her graveside, my mother said, "She's at peace at last."

DEATH BEQUEATHS QUESTIONS. How had Francie unearthed a piece of herself?

In his essay on tragedy, Arthur Miller wrote, "The tragic right is a condition of life, a condition which suppresses man, perverts the flowing out of his love and creative instinct. Tragedy enlightens—and it must, in that it points the heroic finger at the enemy of man's freedom. The thrust for freedom is the quality in tragedy which exalts."

Lobotomy, seen in this light, is arrayed against that freedom; it is anti-tragedy. But when Francie picked up her comb and fixed her hair, when she chose to go down a corridor to say goodbye to Harry, the thrust for freedom reasserted itself in her, and with it the tragedy of her life enlightens—if not her, me.

Then there are the questions about the living. How had my aunts found ways to live with what they'd done? For that matter how do any of us go on after facing up to the damage we've inflicted?

And what if we don't face up? Is there something we can do with guilt so it doesn't just stop inside and start to eat away at our compromised hearts?

3.

17.

I AM DRIVING MY CAR WHEN I HEAR IT, MINNA'S VOICE in my head. I can't write down her words without risking an accident, so I call myself on my cell phone and leave a message on my answering service, speaking words that are coming straight from me and from her—it no longer matters which.

I still don't understand it.

I've tried to look at it from so many angles—here I am an old woman in her seventies and I'm in therapy trying to make sense of what I've done.

You know me, I always wanted to read. And I found time for that, and for my women's lunches ... so why didn't I take the time to find out more about what lobotomy had done to people, to question the doctors more?

I never was any good at standing up to people in authority, I always thought why should they bother with me, I'm a little person to them.

I want to do what my therapist says I should. Be kind to myself. Forgive myself. He keeps saying "we're only human," and "you did the best you could."

But what was I doing sending Francie off to Jen? It was like sending her into a lion's den.

It's like those Nazis, should they be forgiven? Should we say they were "only human"?

Doesn't that make it less, what it means to be human?

"Only human" has to have a higher standard.

I think we couldn't stand it anymore, that there was nothing to be done. Coming up against the awfulness of that—no one wanted to believe that—there had to be something. Maybe time would have been that something? Who knows?

We're all such mysteries to ourselves, aren't we?

JEN SURPRISED EVERYONE, including herself, when she was swept off her feet by Dave, a handsome, silver-haired man who was married to a woman hospitalized for years with Alzheimer's. Dave suggested that Jen live with him in his Florida condo; although The Emily Rose Shoppe had been her life, Jen sold her share of the business to her old lover Moe, ending the connection in her typical businesslike way. The saleswomen, many of whom had worked for her since the store's beginning, cried when she left but were glad she'd found someone.

Minna and my mother didn't approve. They thought he had the makings of a cad. I knew what they meant—I'd seen the way he'd given me the once-over when Jen brought him to meet the family. Then again it couldn't have been easy to run the gauntlet under those loving hawk eyes, older now than when they watched over Dan but still fiercely protective.

When my mother came back after visiting Jen in Florida she reported that Dave treated Jen like a slave, and he flirted with other women beside the pool. But there was more than what my mother saw.

When Jen and Dave went into a Miami restaurant, heads turned to look at them; this tall tanned man with the small elegant woman at his side.

At last she could say to the world, Look, this man has chosen me.

UNDERNEATH HIS GLAMOR, though, Dave wanted someone to take care of him. Jen was not a woman one could see pushing a vacuum cleaner but she tried. She kept on trying, helping him out with cash for a new business venture, getting a face lift after Dave was spotted at Wolfie's Delicatessen with a much younger blonde.

Eventually he told her he had her replacement lined up. My mother flew down to Florida and helped Jen pack, no hesitation, no questions asked. Jen wasn't taking much back in the way of furniture; she'd put most of her good things in storage because Dave hadn't liked them. Ever stoic, Jen walked out of the apartment that she and Dave had shared, leaving no recriminations behind. Her anguish was private and it would be saved for later when she would again surround herself with Persian rugs and the Czech lamps with their dangling crystal prisms.

It was hard for Jen to feel at home in Coolidge Corner, not to be recognized by the new owners of the old family-run shoe store, now one of a chain. Residents from earlier days felt diminished, which was especially hard on Jen, who had been looked up to as the owner of a successful store in her own right.

She went to the movies several times a week, usually to matinees of romantic comedies, until her coughing became so severe that people turned around in their seats. When I would visit, she always had a glass bowl with M&Ms in the center of her coffee table, offering the candies to me, coughing discreetly into her handkerchief. When we both knew I was about to leave, she'd ask, "Are you sure you don't want more?"

I should have asked for more. More about what it had been like to be the young Jen, way ahead of her time, starting her own store. What it had been like to go against convention, how she survived after her disappointments. What it had been like to be the older Jen, needing love, tired of responsibility, wanting something of her own? Beneath her brittle surface was loneliness and despair. But I always thought that Jen was obtuse and, equally obtuse, I went on my way, unaware there would be other questions I'd need to ask in the years ahead.

Jen didn't talk about Francie, and maybe that was all right for her. To acknowledge her role in Francie's destruction might have been unbearable. Sometimes if you want to live, you need to not know.

MINNA WAS A very different person. She wanted to think about everything. Through the years she thought about Leon. She'd wonder aloud to me what her life might have been, had she married her first love.

Then, one day during one of our weekly phone calls, she dropped a bombshell.

"I was walking in Coolidge Corner and you'll never guess what happened. Remember I used to tell you about Leon? The man I wanted to marry, who jilted me? All these years, I never forgot him."

She paused as if momentarily revisiting her own story and went on. "Last week after I left Pick-A-Chick, an old man came up to me, bent over."

She hadn't recognized him. He had to ask whether she remembered him.

"Leon," he'd said. "I'm Leon."

She went through the motions, acknowledging the years since they'd last seen each other. Leon had made his living as an accountant. He had been married for a long time, but his wife died in her late sixties of cancer. He was a widower now, self-respecting in a black and white checked jacket, a handkerchief in pocket.

Shyly he asked whether Minna was still a reader.

"Of course," she replied.

She told him a little bit about the years, but not about Francie. She didn't want him to know the bad stories.

He asked fondly, "Whatever happened to little Pauline?"

Minna filled him in on Pauline's life, the good story.

Then there wasn't all that much more to say, so they said their goodbyes.

I imagine Minna walking home that day, thinking about the things that had happened in her life, about time and passion and change, about Sam who has passed away.

"I always thought I'd feel something if I ever ran into Leon, but I didn't," she is telling herself.

"Poor Bennie. For years I blamed him. He was the reason I lost Leon. But it was never Bennie's fault. It was Leon who wasn't good enough."

Then she is struck with a new thought.

"We were children," I hear her say to herself. "We were what—seventeen, maybe eighteen? Leon was just following what his mother told him to do. That's how we were brought up then. It wasn't his fault either.

"And look what happened. I married Sam with his big booming voice, and the funny thing was he turned out to be a reader, too."

Minna has told me about the letter Sam had left in a drawer for her to read after he died, telling her how he'd never felt worthy of her. How heartbroken she feels that she never told him how much she respected and, yes, loved him.

I see her reaching her building, unlocking her mailbox, and taking out the bills and the magazines, reminding herself to pass the magazines on to the woman down the hall. She takes the elevator up to her apartment, unlocks the door, and goes into the kitchen, where she fills a kettle.

When Minna was nine years old, she'd been quarantined with scarlet fever. She remembers how lonely she felt sleeping in a bed by herself for the first time. Then she looked through the window and there was Jen, her sister, holding an open book to the glass. After Minna read a page, she'd nod, and Jen would turn to the next page. Now Minna takes her cup of tea into the living room and picks up a book from the side table. But tonight she cannot read. She lays the book down.

To the empty room, she says, "I wish you were standing here Francie. I would put my arms around you."

FOR YEARS MINNA and my mother had been after Jen to stop smoking. She couldn't, not even when her emphysema got so bad it kept her confined to the apartment. Minna would get the librarian to put aside books for Jen, seventy years after that first quarantine, the kind of romantic novels Jen liked with vividly illustrated covers—a man and a woman fiercely embracing, as though they were being driven by high winds.

When Jen had to be hooked up to an oxygen tank, it seemed an offense against her nature. To be dependent? To have to draw each breath from a source outside herself?

Jen didn't complain about her illness. She didn't say very much at all, not even when Minna and my mother, who had been visiting every day, began to come twice a day.

One day they walked through the apartment, turning off the lamps. The crystal prisms that once had sounded against each other were stilled.

Do you love me? The question that always lay just under Jen's shell had been answered by her sisters. Yes.

THE HABIT OF the goodnight phone call doesn't go away easily, and now Minna and my mother are both grateful for it. There is no longer a pot that bubbles, no need for a spoon to stir.

My mother had done the unexpected: she let go.

About Bennie, she said, "Sometimes there's no choice." All she'd say about Francie was, "It shouldn't have happened. But what's done is done." Her old answer, the one that to me had sounded as though she were shutting off possibility, held her in good stead those last years, reconciling her to what couldn't be changed.

She remained elegant, the way she put herself together admired by the nurses at the nursing home where eventually she had to live. The years were cruel to her; she lost a leg. But her armor—the high value she placed on the material world, which I'd always thought she overvalued—had become so much a part of her that it sustained her in those last years. Bennie was a memory seldom revisited; everything that happened to Francie was terribly sad but it didn't stab her with guilt.

To the end, she was interested in other people, becoming friendly with the nurses, sending me their recipes for chicken in red wine and cranberry bread with walnuts. She wasn't happy, but she didn't suffer from the particular unhappiness that comes from being tormented by the past.

SHE LEFT ME with the greenness she once had offered on her palm. The open pod of peas. Mmmm. We agreed, so sweet.

MINNA LIVED TO be a very old woman, enjoying her nightly Hoodsie. She lived long enough to become querulous, to pinch pennies so that she'd have enough money to leave to Dan. Even though she knew he lived comfortably, she still worried about him.

She was ninety-seven and had seen the beginning of a new century when Dan phoned to tell me to come to the nursing home.

By the time I got there, she had slipped into a coma. In profile she looked so much like my mother—the same silvery hair back from the forehead, the same beaky nose. But the resemblance was more than feature by feature. It was family, as though everything had been stripped away at the end but the features that linked them.

I lay down beside her and put my head on her pillow.

I thought about her pain at what had happened to Francie and, at these last moments, wanted to relieve her of it in the only way I know, with the truth as I understand it.

To this aunt of all my years, I said, "We all fail each other in the short run. It's the long run that matters."

She remained still, eyes closed.

I whispered, "I will always have my arms around you."

I put my cheek against hers for the last time.

18.

SO FAR I'VE STAYED INSIDE THE MARGINS OF THE STORIES
I'd been told, the events I've experienced.

But now I have to face up to it: I haven't directly confronted the question my visit with Pauline raised—was Bennie schizophrenic? If there's more information to be had, it will have to come
from someone outside the family.

But who is left? Only as I search for a more distant perspective, do I see how little was ever outside the family. The circle that
the sisters created as little girls against the hurled blueberries and
the flung spinach had swung inward and closed, opening only to
try to bring us, the resistant children, into it.

DR. MYERSON'S SON? Would he remember Bennie?

I try Massachusetts Information.

No such person listed.

Is he still alive?

I call a friend who lives in Boston and ask her to look him up
in the local phone book. No, not there either.

I'm off the hook. If truth be told, I'd prefer not encountering
him again. There's too much history between us. But isn't that the
point of needing to talk with him?

I google him, and sure enough, there are several people with
the same name, one listed as a resident of a retirement community in Arizona. Maybe Dr. Myerson has migrated to dry air? I phone,
but no one there has heard of anyone by that name.

I remember a distant cousin related to the Myersons; can I track him down? Yes, and he has the information I need. The younger Myerson, now in his eighties, is alive and well and living in Florida.

Before I phone, I review a few sentences that I've jotted down to reintroduce myself: "I'm the niece of ... "

He remembers me. At least my name. And yes, my family.

"I don't understand exactly what you want," he replies with a reserve I still remember, "but I'll try to be as helpful as I can."

What I want from him is an incontrovertible answer.

"Did you know my uncle Bennie?"

"I met him a few times, and my father used to talk to me about him."

"Before the lobotomy?"

"No." He answers with a bit of impatience as if to say I'm not that old. "But don't forget I knew about your family through my father, and then through my first wife."

"Was there any chance at all," I ask, "that Bennie could have been misdiagnosed? That he wasn't schizophrenic?"

"Where did you ever get such an idea? There's no question about it. Your uncle was a chronic schizophrenic."

Here it is. The younger Myerson has confirmed what I always believed.

All along I had thought I'd feel jubilant when I heard that answer, but instead I feel hollow. Perhaps this is no longer the most important question.

"Do you remember," I ask, "how his lobotomy came about?"

"My father was involved in making that decision. When lobotomy became an option, he thought it was for the greater good of society. He liked to do what we now call cost-benefit analysis. In Bennie's case, he must have thought it was the right thing for him, and for the good of the family."

"Was Bennie better off post-lobotomy?"

"He was the classic case—erratically violent—and lobotomy tamed him."

"What did you think about lobotomy?"

"I thought it had no curative value whatsoever. Hospitals were on a kick, using it to quiet people. I was interning at Mass. Mental Health in the forties, and I'd see people sent over to Mass. General for the surgery. When they came back it was appalling."

"Why didn't you speak up," I ask, "if you thought it shouldn't have been done?"

There's a pause, so long it becomes uncomfortable.

"Would you excuse me," he says, "while I get some ginger ale? My throat is dry."

I wait, hearing an old man's footsteps and then the clink of ice near the receiver. I ask my question again, rephrasing it so that it doesn't sound like an accusation.

He replies, "My father was all for it, and he was a formidable man. He could make me feel like I was this high. When I was a boy, he tried to teach me about socialism and I yawned. He said, "I'm talking above your head.""

I ask him whether that bothered him.

"It must have, I still remember it."

"Do you remember Francie? My aunt who had the lobotomy?"

"I do indeed. She was a highly neurotic woman whose life was terribly sad."

I ask him what he thinks about my idea that Francie had suffered from abandonment depression, that her unappeasable pain had been inflicted long before Harry.

"Your interpretation makes sense, but what happened, happened. One can try to look back for causes, but who really knows? That's the mystery."

I don't tell him that I think he's got hold of the wrong mystery. "What happened, happened" doesn't get us anywhere. It's like throwing up one's hands and letting the past spread behind us, a blob without meaning. To me, there are greater mysteries: how Francie could have risen to her moment, how Bennie could have written his note with the words, "I hope."

"Would she have been helped if she were alive now, with all the new drugs?

"Probably not," he answers. "It was a severe case of agitated anxiety. The new drugs do not, for the most part, work for people at that level."

He doesn't seem open to further speculation. But I don't buy it; too much has changed for him to dismiss any advance out of hand. I wish—a lot—that she could have tried them, even knowing that my dream of rescue may be just that, a dream, but that I prefer to err on the side of possibility.

"You do know that my father discovered the first antidepressant?"

Yes, I do know. The elder Myerson had brought a new formulation and a new category into the diagnostic criteria for depression; he called it anhedonia. In *Jews and the American Soul: Human Nature in the Twentieth Century*, Andrew R. Heinze has written, "Convinced of the purposefulness of existence even without any divine foundation ... Myerson put the traditional religious problem of despair onto the psychiatric map when he introduced the concept of anhedonia."

In Myerson, the man and the thinker, a European despair was counteracted by an Emersonian belief in vitality and self-reliance. He wrote, "Life, to be worth the living, must have its enthusiasms, must swing constantly from desire to satisfaction, or else seems void and painful."

His new drug was called Benzedrine, later to become known as "bennies." It did re-enthuse people with that zest for life that Myerson extolled: Jack Kerouac wrote *On the Road* in three weeks under its influence; Malcolm X found it useful, as did James Bond, as well as college students like myself, who took speed to stay up all night. Myerson didn't live to know that the chemical structure of the stimulant he championed would be closely to methamphetamine. We know not what we do.

"But it turned out to be addictive," I say.

His son is a little defensive. "No one knows the long-term effects of these new drugs."

I ask him the question I've been holding back.

"Back then, were you worried about me? Did you think I was crazy?"

"I wasn't worried, and you shouldn't have been either. You were confused and lost, but underneath you knew what you were doing. You were unhappy. But it was nothing that you couldn't solve in time."

He must hear the relief on my exhale. He wants to know how I found my way.

"Resilience and luck," I tell him and plunge on: "and I take antidepressants. They've helped me enormously."

I remember when I made an appointment to see a psychiatrist because I was depressed. By the time I got to see him, my natural resilience had lifted me back up. I told him as much, adding, "The only thing that's still bothering me is how hard it is for me to write. I come up against a boulder in the road and the only way to get past it is by pushing with all my strength." Then I said, "But no pill can help with that." I'll never forget his eyebrow arching into a circumflex "Oh no?" he said.

The boulder did disappear. It still comes back from time to time—no one gets that lucky. But I no longer push. I wait it out for a few days, knowing it will eventually pulverize, if not today then the next. At a panel on my work, another writer asked me, "What do you do about despair?" I was amazed; I had never heard a question like that asked openly in front of several hundred people. Without thinking, I said, "Pills." After the slightly embarrassed audience giggle, I went on. "Frankly, even if I knew I'd become addicted, I'd go on taking them, that's how much better my life is."

To the younger Myerson I now say, "I just hope that people won't look back someday and think they're barbaric ... "

"Pills are reversible," he says, making the implicit comparison to lobotomy.

He goes on while inside I have stopped, hearing myself ...

barbaric ... an echo of the time when my family made its choices, an affirmation of the timelessness of our dilemmas.

"I just hope ... "

I thank the doctor for his time. We say goodbye politely, knowing we will not speak again.

DAN AND I speak every month or so just to catch up with each other. To my surprise, he has returned to Boston, after first retiring from broadcasting and going on to live the life of a gentleman farmer in Connecticut. I was the only one who knew he began each day by going to his study in the barn and writing his secret novels. But when his wife became ill, he decided to put his trust in Boston's medical expertise.

Now he is alone, staying on, cantankerous, to this day unwilling to admit that he keeps up with what's left of the family, which at this point is Pauline, still protecting himself so that no one can break into his shell, which after seventy years remains both strong and vulnerable. He has, however, opened up some. In the last few years he has let me read his books—and to my immense pleasure and relief, they're good.

This time Dan is calling to tell me that Pauline's kidneys are failing. He reminisces: "You know, when I was a kid I loved Pauline. She was fun, spirited, always interested in what I was doing." She has, he tells me, decided against dialysis, opting instead for the supposedly gentle death of kidney failure.

Should I go back? I don't ever want to hear her accusations again.

When I phone Pauline to tell her I'm coming, she says, "I'm going to hold my breath until you get here." I know she is only being effusive but I have to admit that it feels good to be wanted. Besides, I too am holding my breath.

I've been preparing for this to be my final visit, expecting her to be on her last legs. But no. I knock at the door of her apartment and there she is, the last aunt, greeting me in white slacks and a flowered blouse, agile as she bends down to the lowest shelf of the refrigerator to get me orange juice that I do not want but feel obliged to take after saying no to coffeecake, cheese, and fruit.

She fills me in on her failing energy. "I wish I could have gone on leading my discussion group on Emily Dickinson. I miss doing that."

As always with Pauline, she delivers an unexpected blow.

Having applauded my earlier memoir about the last years of my parents' lives, she now pounces when I tell her that I'm writing a new book about the lobotomies in our family.

"Put it in a drawer. Forget it."

"Why should I want to do that?"

"Lots of writers put things away in drawers."

I happen to know that Pauline has written stories that have not seen the light of day. Maybe it's frustration that makes her want to bury me in that drawer with her.

I don't try to come back at her other than to say, "I can't do that, Pauline. I want other people to read what I write."

"But you're writing to feel better about it," Pauline says. "Isn't that enough?"

"No, that's not why I write. Writing isn't a way to feel better. I only wish it were."

"Then why are you writing it?"

"Because I'm a person who needs to find things out and tries to make sense of them."

I add, just to underline that we share some things, "And because I have the writing gene, the same one Minna had and you have."

No hiss this time at Minna's name.

I had come there wanting to tell her that the younger Dr. Myerson had confirmed that Bennie had been a chronic schizophrenic. But what's the point? She's too old and I'm too tired to argue about who's right, who's wrong, even what's true and what's false. Dr. Myerson had called Bennie "erratically violent"—maybe Pauline had chosen to remember him when he wasn't violent and distance had allowed her to keep those memories intact.

Out of the blue she wants to talk about my grandmother, how I'd never appreciated her. "She liked to dance and sing." Pauline shows me a story she'd written years ago with a wonderful line: she calls her mother "the belle of the ball on a leaky ship." The story recounts my grandmother's passage to America when she was in steerage with other immigrants, living on herring and stale bread. Pauline wrote that the first-class passengers caught a glimpse of her dancing and brought her to the upper deck, giving her extra food that she brought down to her famished cohort below. I don't say anything but I have a feeling I've seen this movie. Oh well. It was written by a young Pauline who wanted to tell of the good, shown to me now by a dying woman who wants to claim pride in her family.

Then in typical Pauline fashion, she veers. This is the Pauline paradox, the dissonance that has always stood in the way of my seeing her clearly: at a moment's notice she goes from reserves of mind and spirit to the malice she has shown about her family. Then she flips back to her best self, but just when I see her as wonderful she swerves into vitriol.

Now she is eager to tell me a new story. "Harry drugged Francie and then he called Minna and said Francie was acting crazy and she should take her to the hospital. Harry lied all the time. He was always trying to put Francie into mental hospitals."

"Why," I ask with trepidation, "did Harry do this?"

"He wanted out."

A husband drugging his wife, putting her away in a mental hospital ... Harry certainly wanted out, but this scenario sounds like a 1940s movie. Maybe she should have been a screenwriter.

And indeed, she goes on to tell me that she has an idea for a screenplay. Yes, this always intelligent, sometimes spiteful woman who will soon die has a new career in mind.

"I've got an idea for a story ... "

Oh Pauline ...

Her idea is based on a time when she and her husband had volunteered at The Walter E. Fernald School, established in 1848 as the Massachusetts School for the Feeble-Minded, later renamed for Fernald, its third superintendent who was an advocate for eugenics. As CBS' *60 Minutes* reported in 2004, "A large proportion of the kids who were locked up there were not retarded at all. They were simply poor, uneducated kids with no place to go."

The movie she would like to write is based on a story told to her by one of her favorite boys, Fred Boyce, who still visits Pauline from time to time. When he was a baby, he'd been abandoned by his mother, dropped off at the school, getting out only by escaping. He was a young man sitting at the counter of a coffee shop when he had a sudden powerful sense that he knew the waitress—knew her beyond acquaintance, beyond likeness to another person, but in a deep inexplicable way. Years later, when he traced his family, he discovered that the waitress had been his own mother.

It's a hell of a story. A child abandoned, unjustly labeled and locked up in an evil school. It even has a bit of extrasensory perception in the service of the mysterious bonds of family. But there's a darker story yet. Some forty years after Fred Boyce left The Fernald School, he blew the whistle on an experiment in which he'd taken part, one of a group of boys recruited as test subjects for an experiment conducted by MIT researchers. The boys were told they were special, that they had been selected to belong to a Science Club and given a few extra privileges, in exchange—and this they were not told—for their lives. Quaker Oats wanted to trace the absorption of cereal into the body and had contracted with the university and the school to feed the boys radioactive oatmeal.

Fred Boyce is dying of his exposure to radiation.

In the past when I'd read about medical experimentation on human subjects, I'd thought about eugenics, Josef Mengele, Tuskegee, and HeLa cells. Once again, though, the wide world with all its sorrows had spiraled down to touch my family. Pauline tells me that when she was a volunteer there the school was considered a model institution, and although she was close with several of the boys, none of them had said anything about the experiments. Nor had she known about the other atrocities—the sexual abuse, the solitary confinement. The boys had been told they must never tell.

Soon, she says, a book will be published that tells the whole story. I must look a little skeptical because she goes over to her desk and pulls out an article in a national weekly magazine. It's true: Pauline has known boys who were considered as expendable as the women who had been sterilized by the eugenicists, as the asylum inmates on whom Moniz had performed his first operations, as Rosemary Kennedy, the inconvenient daughter. Pauline tells me that she has been interviewed for the book. She who has told doubtful stories has become part of the great project of speaking truth.

I beg off at eleven thirty at night, tired. She has worn me out. Unfolding the sofa bed already made up for me, I look over to the bench under the picture window expecting to see the dollhouse that she and her husband made. Instead there's an empty space.

I call out to Pauline in her bedroom.

"What happened to the dollhouse?"

She tells me that she donated it to a children's museum, arranging for them to come for it when she knew she was dying. Last week she notified the museum to pick it up.

THE NEXT DAY Pauline sleeps until midday. I look into her bedroom and see what looks like a doll on the bed, a miniature version of my aunt lying on her back, wearing a robe that comes down to her knees, exposing her small ragdoll legs. It is no miniature, no doll. It is my aunt, seen unguarded. I understand: yesterday she had assembled herself for her guest. For me.

I wait, hoping Pauline will wake up so that I can say goodbye, nervous, though, because I have to catch a plane. I look again at my watch and see that it really is time to leave.

She opens her eyes, bends her arm at the elbow. She looks up at me. Winks. Waves. Goodbye.

ON THAT EARLIER visit to Pauline, I walked out onto the residence's village green and dismissed it as an ersatz Colonial fantasy. Now I look again and see it as well-tended order, a stop against final chaos.

I drive the car back to the airport and board my flight home, back to California. In the plane I think about Pauline. Split souls, we all have them, whether they are conjoined twins or completely divided. In the past, I saw Pauline as the one who'd escaped the wounds of her other sisters, but now I think her wounds were so deep she has never recovered. I have been audience to a grand performance, her damages bandaged with a combination of spite and grace. Grace she had to find for herself.

We are beginning our descent into Los Angeles. As twilight turns to dusk and lights are beginning to go on in the tall buildings down below, I feel that old squeeze at my heart. This time I greet THE FEELING as an old friend because I know now that the little girl who had been standing on the porch all those years ago hadn't been sick. She had been alive, open to the complex shadings around her, responding to all the ways that people come home at the end of their days. I had felt their griefs and exaltations as my own. THE FEELING belonged not to pathology but to poetry. To the fullness of life.

From the window seat I hear the wheels locking, see the landing gear lowering. Down below, neon signs are springing up on Century Boulevard, and there are lights now in bungalows on their narrow lots. The memory of my father's failed stores rises up to meet me, the lights bringing home the valor of aspiration, of trying hard to make a home, a business, a life, all of us living with struggle and looking for grace.

19.

BACK IN MY OWN HOME, I TELL MY HUSBAND WHAT PAULINE
has said, that I shouldn't be writing this book. I need his advice:
am I raking over cold coals?

To answer my question, he needs to read the book. But this
is this book, where I write the story of my plagiarism. I still have
never told anyone about it, afraid of people realizing I'm not the
person they thought I was, afraid of disappointing my husband.

He takes the manuscript into the next room. When he's done,
he doesn't talk about whether I should be writing this book, only
about what he liked and what he thinks isn't working yet.

"But what," I ask, "about my plagiarizing the paper?"

He says, "Everyone does stuff like that when they're young."

It's almost laughable, isn't it, if it hadn't been so awful—
decades of carrying around an adolescent girl, thinking I was still
that person? How many people must feel the same way about their
pasts, still feeling shame, not realizing that as we grow older, our
trespasses can deflate?

But just because my husband let me off the hook, I don't
want to give myself a blanket amnesty. There's no question about
it: I should have confessed back then to the plagiarism. And Minna
should have saved Francie. Our motives, our selves, are all mixed,
I know that. But that's not enough either. For too long I've lived on
a bridge with stanchions at each end: one is blame and the other
is exoneration, but neither has afforded a broad view. The bridge I
am looking for allows for a crossing and a path beyond.

MINNA HAS TOLD me a story that takes me to that path. It happened on that terrible day more than eighty years ago when Bennie hurt Dan. Sam had a bad temper; all day long she had been dreading what he might do when he came home from work and found out what her brother had done.

Sam walked over to Bennie, who was standing a little distance away.

"What did you do to my son?" Sam asked in a puzzled voice. "How could you have hurt my boy?"

Bennie didn't say anything. He turned his hand palm up to show Sam a scratch on the inside of his own wrist.

Sam saw the mark, shook his head and walked away.

Later that night, he told Minna that he understood Bennie to be saying, "I feel so bad about what I did to Dan that I punished myself. I hurt my own arm."

Although Sam seems almost unbelievably saintly in this story, I choose to believe it because it speaks to what I have been searching for. Sam understood that he too belonged to the family, and had he raged at Bennie he would have torn the delicate fabric of which he was a part.

It was more than that, though, something stronger than anger, stronger even than justice.

Sam offered Bennie the mercy of fellow feeling, the mercy that is owed to family and to the human family, and, finally, the mercy that is owed to oneself. It is what allows the troubled child to translate pain into art. It is what turns a person in the direction of grace.

MYSTERIES DON'T GO away by themselves, at least not in my experience; they demand attention, clamoring for the starring role. Bennie's get well note: was he capable of writing it himself? Was he able to hope that something would happen in the future, when the idea of a future wasn't supposed to be available to him?

I tracked down a psychologist at the University of California who studies changes that occur when people undergo frontal lobe injuries. I phoned Dr. Klein and told him about Bennie's note. His first response was, "How much of your uncle's personal memories were attacked?" He explained that he was referring to one particular kind of memory, which he called episodic; a person with episodic memory knows he has experienced an event at a particular time.

I answered that Bennie seemed to know that our family Thanksgivings had happened and that he had been there.

Klein asked, "But does this mean that he *owns* the experience, that he knows he has a self that does the experiencing?"

"How would I even guess," I asked him, "whether Bennie did or didn't know he was Bennie?"

"Your uncle would have to have had the ability for self-reflection, a sense that he himself caused things to happen."

"I'm almost positive that Bennie couldn't reflect, certainly not about himself. Wait—he used to complain about kids following him from the barbershop and making fun of him. Does that count?"

"Did he express any feelings about it? Did he ever seem hurt by their behavior? Did he say he'd like to do something to them in return?"

"I've always assumed he felt upset by it because he said it a number of times. But that's me, isn't it, making the connection? I never saw anything to indicate that he was angry or wanted to retaliate, or that he ever realized he could make something happen."

"For Bennie to realize that, he'd have to understand time as it unfolds and as a series of personal happenings that centered around himself."

I doubt that Bennie's sense of time was anything like what he had just described.

"That's critical," he said, "because it's the experience of self-continuity that provides the mental scaffolding from which we can imagine possible future states—states in which we ourselves might be involved."

So.

That's it.

Bennie couldn't have stood on that scaffolding, looked ahead to a future with himself in it, and hoped that it would happen.

And yet.

Dr. Klein had asked whether Bennie owned his experience.

I ask myself whether I own my experience.

No, since I feel quite sure that experience is what one cannot own.

ONCE I HAD stood still on a village green of a nursing home, asking myself what I should do about Pauline's accusations. I tried to appease the sleeping dog inside me, pat him, tiptoe away, and leave everyone to her own experience, her own private possession. But the dog lifted his head, sniffed, and ventured out into that hour between twilight and dusk when, across long distances, dogs exchange barks and we exchange words.

I look at Bennie's note once more, closer now, at the labored writing and the crossed-out words. I can feel the pressure of Bennie's pen, the concentration he brought to the task, his struggle to get a word right.

The psychologist had held up self-continuity as the essential requirement for being able to imagine the future. But self-continuity isn't all that we claim for it.

Bennie had *other*-continuity. He had been present throughout much of his adult life at our annual family Thanksgivings, always at the same house and with the same people, their familiarity becoming the "other."

When Bennie wrote his note, it was long before we knew our brains possess a beautiful plasticity that fills the spaces left by loss and also allows for change; we know now that experience itself can spark new neural pathways. Somewhere in Bennie's fragmented brain, I imagine those pathways were strengthened each time our family Thanksgivings recurred, giving Bennie elements of continuity. Not as an individual self who feels his centrality to an event, but as an event in which others had participated and might again.

I had asked the wrong question when I wondered how Bennie might have a sense of the future. Hope isn't about the future. It's the friend of our present, a biological and spiritual intervention against obliteration. Hope, or *hopes*. Why should hope not have its own varieties? Why should time not imprint us all, in its own ways, with our own thanksgivings?

ONCE MORE I take out the 1915 photograph. I look at Minna, Jen, Helen, and Pauline, at Bennie before the demons began to speak to him, at Francie too young for the photograph but there nonetheless.

These little girls made a circle. It helped them survive, gave their lives meaning, and trapped them. Their love for one another sat side by side with their failures and weaknesses.

Only now I can answer Pauline's question, Why are you writing this book?

To find my way to loving you with your tragic mistakes, your wounds, your passions, your pity, your love, to feel in my heart the meaning of Bennie's words, the ones he wrote to me in his own hand.

I hope we will all be together again

Timeline

1904 Minna is born.

1905 Jen is born.

1909 Bennie is born.

1911 Helen is born.

1914 Pauline is born.

1915 Family photograph is taken.

1920 Francie is born.

1923 Bennie begins to act strangely.

1925 Myerson's first visit.

1926 Father leaves.

1926 Minna and Sam marry.

1930 Dan (Minna's son) is born.

1932 Helen and Lou (my parents) marry.

1933 Pauline and George marry.

1934 Bennie attacks Dan.

1935 The First Neurological Congress, in London.

1935–36 Egas Moniz performs "leucotomy," the first brain surgery to treat mental illness.

1936–37 Walter Freeman modifies Moniz's procedure, renaming it "lobotomy."

1938 Jen opens Emily Rose Shoppe.

1939 Myerson returns to the apartment of Minna and Sam. In Japan, the first lobotomy is performed; it will be used extensively in mental hospitals.

1940 Bennie undergoes a lobotomy.

1941 John F. Kennedy's sister, Rosemary, is lobotomized by Walter Freeman. Francie marries Harry.

1942 Publication of Freeman and Watts's book on psychosurgery, *Psychosurgery. Intelligence, Emotion and Social Behavior Following Prefrontal Lobotomy for Mental Disorders.*

1943 Harry enters the army. Tennessee Williams's sister, Rose, is lobotomized. I am born.

1944 *The Glass Menagerie* opens in Chicago.

1945 Freeman performs the first transorbital lobotomy.

1947 Allen Ginsberg's mother, Naomi, is lobotomized.

1948 Abraham Myerson dies.

1949 Egas Moniz wins Nobel Prize for lobotomy.

1950–54 Walter Freeman sets out in his Lobotomobile barnstorming America.

1951 On the waiting list for a lobotomy, New Zealand author Janet Frame wins the Hubert Church Award for best prose. Frame said, "I repeat that my writing saved me." Later nominated for a Nobel Prize in Literature.

1953 Francie and Harry move in with Jen.

1954 Introduction of Thorazine, a pharmaceutical treatment for schizophrenia that begins to signal the end for lobotomy.

1955 Harry leaves marriage. Egas Moniz dies.

1955 Francie's first suicide attempt.

1956 Naomi Ginsberg dies.

1957 Grandma dies.

1955–58 Francie's hospitalizations and electric shock therapy.

1958 Francie's lobotomy.

1962 Publication of *One Flew Over the Cuckoo's Nest* by Ken Kesey; becomes a classic.

1964 Publication of *Sanity, Madness and the Family* by R.D. Laing; controversial claim that disorders arise from experiences within the family and therefore should not be considered mental diseases.

1967 Bennie dies.

1967 Walter Freeman performs his last lobotomy.

1970   Publication of book *Violence and the Brain* with its suggestion that lobotomy be used for social control.

1970s Lobotomy falls into disrepute in Japan partly due to its use on children with behavioral problems. This was a general pattern that would be repeated in other countries in the years ahead, although its use in China is as yet unknown.

1972   Reports of surgery on prisoners; topic became a civil rights issue.

1972   Legislation restricting psychosurgery enacted on a state-by-state basis.

1973   Death of Francie.

1974   Legal suit brought to stop state hospitals from continuing to do lobotomies.

1975   Film of *One Flew Over the Cuckoo's Nest* wins five major Academy Awards; public sees image of lobotomy used for institutional control.

1975   Jen sells her share of the Emily Rose Shoppe to Moe and goes to Florida.

1978–79 Decline in numbers of psychosurgeries.

1986 Jen returns.

1988 I move to California.

1989 Introduction of new antipsychotic medications; Clozaril proves effective.

1994 Death of Jen.

1998 Moe's son tapes this note to the shuttered windows of the Emily Rose Shoppe:

> *"THANK YOU!!! for all the 59 years of WONDERFUL Friendships— Hope to see you in the future! PLEASE MAIL PAYMENTS (Return envelopes provided)."*

2001 Death of Minna.

2002 First visit to Pauline.

2005 Second visit to Pauline.

2006 Death of Pauline. Death of Fred Boyce.

1980–Ongoing Psychosurgery returns in different ways: deep brain stimulation by implanting electrodes on the brain's surface as treatment for Parkinson's disease; cingulotomies to treat extreme depression and obsessive compulsive disorder. Ongoing debate.

Development of neurobioethics as a discipline; neuroethics committees in hospitals to review individual cases.

Informed consent continues to be violated in studies using human beings.

Soma vs. psyche on the way to being resolved by new technologies, among them scans that can predict whether therapy or medication is the preferred treatment for an individual patient.

Lobotomy as warning against indifference. A lobotomy is a permanent disconnect; ours doesn't have to be.

2013   A Wall Street Journal report reveals that the Veterans Administration lobotomized 2,000 veterans in the 1940s and 1950s.

A list of sources consulted

Adler, Alexandra. *Guiding Human Misfits: A Practical Application of Individual Psychology*. New York: Macmillan, 1938.

Andreasen, Nancy C. *Brave New Brain: Conquering Mental Illness in the Era of the Genome*. Oxford: Oxford University Press, 2001.

Braslow, Joel. *Mental Ills and Bodily Cures*. Berkeley: University of California Press, 1997.

Carrere, Emmanuel. *Lives Other Than My Own*. New York: Metropolitan Books, 2009.

Charon, Rita, and Martha Montello. *Stories Matter: The Role of Narrative in Medical Ethics*. New York: Routledge, 2002.

Damasio, Antonio. *Descartes' Error: Emotion, Reason, and the Human Brain*. New York: Avon Books, 1994.

———. *Self Comes to Mind: Constructing the Conscious Brain*. New York: Pantheon Books, 2010.

———. *The Feeling of What Happens: Body and Emotion in the Making of Consciousness*. New York: Houghton Mifflin Harcourt, 1999.

D'Antonio, Michael. *The State Boys Rebellion*. New York: Simon & Schuster, 2004.

El-hai, Jack. *The Lobotomist*. Hoboken, NJ: Wiley, 2005.

Ginsberg, Allen. *Kaddish and Other Poems*. San Francisco: City Lights, 1961.

———. *White Shroud*. New York: Harper & Row, 1986.

Goldberg, Elkhonon. *The Executive Brain: Frontal Lobes and the Civilized Mind*. Oxford: Oxford University Press, 2001.

Groopman, Jerome. *The Anatomy of Hope*, Reprint ed. New York: Random House, 2005.

Heinze, Andrew R. *Jews and the American Soul*. Princeton, NJ: Princeton University Press, 2004.

Karp, David A. *The Burden of Sympathy: How Families Cope with Mental Illness*. Oxford: Oxford University Press, 2001.

Klein, Stanley B. *The Two Selves: Their Metaphysical Commitments and Functional Independence*. Oxford: Oxford University Press, 2013.

Laing, R.D. *The Divided Self*. London: Penguin, 1969.

Lakoff, George, and Mark Johnson. *Philosophy in The Flesh*. New York: Basic Books, 1999.

Leverich, Lyle. *Tom: the Unknown Tennessee Williams*. New York: Norton, 1995.

Margalit, Avishai. *The Decent Society*. Cambridge, MA: Harvard University Press, 1996.

———. *The Ethics of Memory*. Cambridge, MA: Harvard University Press, 2002.

Miller, Alice. *The Untouched Key: Tracing Childhood Trauma in Creativity and Destructiveness*. New York: Anchor Books, 1990.

Miles, Barry. *Ginsberg: A Biography*. New York: Simon & Schuster, 1989.

Morris, David B. *Illness and Culture in the Postmodern Age*. Berkeley: University of California Press, 1998.

Myerson, Abraham. *Speaking of Man*. New York: Knopf, 1950.

———. *The Nervous Housewife*. Boston: Little, Brown, 1920.

Neiman, Susan. *Evil in Modern Thought: An Alternative History of Philosophy*. Princeton, NJ: Princeton University Press, 2002.

Neugeboren, Jay. *Imagining Robert: A Memoir*. New Brunswick, NJ: Rutgers University Press, 1997.

———. *Transforming Madness*. Los Angeles: University of California Press, 2001.

Pressman, Jack D. *Last Resort: Psychosurgery and the Limits of Medicine*. Cambridge: Cambridge University Press, 1998.

Rasmussen, Nicolas. *On Speed: The Many Lives of Amphetamine*. New York: NYU Press, 2008.

Solomon, Andrew. *Far From the Tree: Parents, Children and the Search for Identity*. New York: Simon & Schuster, 2012. Kindle e-book.

Tejada. Susan. *In Search of Sacco and Vanzetti: Double Lives, Troubled Times, and the Massachusetts Murder Case That Shook the World*. Boston: Northeastern University Press, 2012.

Valenstein, Elliot S. *Great and Desperate Cures: The Rise and Decline of Psychosurgery and Other Radical Treatments for Mental Illness*. New York: Basic Books, 1986.

Williams, Dakin, and Shepherd Mead. *Tennessee Williams: An Intimate Biography*. Gettysburg, PA: Arbor House, 1983.

Williams, Tennessee, Albert J. Devlin, and Nancy Marie Patterson Tischler. *The Selected Letters of Tennessee Williams, Volume 1: 1920-1945*. New York: New Directions, 2002.

Williams, Tennessee, Albert J. Devlin, and Nancy Marie Patterson Tischler. *The Selected Letters of Tennessee Williams, Volume 2: 1945-1957*. New York: New Directions, 2004.

Williams, Tennessee. *The Glass Menagerie: Acting Edition*. New York: Dramatists Play Service, 1998.

Acknowledgements

FIRST OF ALL, GREAT THANKS TO MY HUSBAND, STEVEN D. Lavine, who is also my best friend, and whose astute and deep comments, made after each of many readings, live on in the veins and arteries of this book.

Great thanks to my agent, Gail Hochman, who read and reread this book, making it better by her insights and by keeping the faith—gifts every writer needs and wants. Pride of place for exceptional insights, repeated readings, and enthusiastic long-term belief goes to Philip Alexis Littell, Jörn Jacob Rohwer, and bookseller extraordinaire Doug Dutton.

For help of every sort, all of it marked by perceptive thought and generosity of spirit, I give thanks to Perry Miller Adato, Betsy Amster, Marisa Canales, Jo Ann Callis, Steve Erickson and his colleagues at *Black Clock*, Sonya Friedman, Bette Korman, Richard Metzner, Travis Preston, Marissa Chibas Preston, John Rechy and the members of his workshop, Ladette Randolph, Robert Schnitzer, Jane St. Clair, and Zoune Lasseure.

Each book has its own community, enlarging now to include early readers of drafts and all-around good people who helped more than they know: Barbara Abrash, Frank Alva Buecheler, Mario Garcia, Rafael Lopez-Barrantes, Nannette Mongelluzo, Gina Nahai, Lori Precious, Judith Searle and the Enneagram, Carol Tavris, Daisy Vreeland, and the spirited and supportive members of the Women's Lunch Group.

A special thanks goes to Jana Harris, who lit the match that started this book; after reading my earlier book *Phantom Limb*, she said, "Now I want to know about the sisters." I owe a special debt to Hawthorne Books' publisher, Rhonda Hughes, for realizing that a book about a difficult subject could and should be brought into the world, and then doing a superb job of publishing it; and to Hawthorne's senior editor, Adam O'Connor Rodriguez, every writer's dream editor, whose sensitivity and acumen have been essential to the book's realization.

Thanks to my family for sharing memories and images, with special gratitude to Michael B. Katz, Diane Somerset Miller, and Joseph B. Somerset; to Dr. David Myerson for our conversation, whose spirit and sense I have tried to convey; also to Stanley B. Klein for sharing with me his theories of self; to Timothy Corrigan for the use of his splendid Paris apartment, where I wrote several drafts, and to the University of Granada's Residence, which provided the setting for several more drafts. I'm also sending appreciation to my colleagues at the California Institute of the Arts, most especially for the example of their dedication to their work; and to Sally, dog of my heart, who was at my side for most of the years I spent writing this book.

White Matter is dedicated to Herman Engel, dear friend of many years unmarked by anything but the pleasure of each other's company; how I wish he could read this final version.

An Interview with Janet Sternburg

Adam O'Connor Rodriguez

Senior Editor, Hawthorne Books
November 2014

ADAM O'CONNOR RODRIGUEZ: *What did the writing process look like for this book?*

JANET STERNBURG: I'm slow—*White Matter* took eleven years, and the number of revisions was in the three figures. I felt that life had given me an incredible story only I could tell, and I'd better honor it by going into it as thoroughly as possible. I needed history, neurobiology, psychology, philosophy, and family stories to begin to make sense of it.

Then I had to figure out how to tell it—words, sentences, structure, white space, flow—all those things that for me at least require trying, and then trying again. Some people I know questioned how and why I kept going. I came up with an answer: The book presented the problems to me that were the most interesting ones to solve. At times I was in love with what I was writing, and like all kinds of love, it makes it impossible to stay away.

Writers tend to quantify the number of years a book takes without qualifying what else was happening during that time. The long slog becomes artificially heroic. But I've always been various and curious: I enjoy moving back and forth between a number of projects. During the years I spent writing *White Matter*, I also became a serious photographer, a play I wrote was produced, I shattered my ankle. While I was recovering from that injury, I came up with an idea (never put into practice) for a vanity license plate: WRK SVS U (Work Saves You). I believe it.

Now, I confess, I'm hoping to write something lighthearted that just pours out of me. If only …

AOR: White Matter *required a lot of research, and some of that research is woven into the text. How did you research the book, and how did you make decisions about what research to include?*

JS: I'm sure there are methods known to scholars with PhDs, but I'm not trained that way.

Reading is what's natural for me. I grew up reading books under the covers; they were my security blanket. I still go to sleep with a book in my hand, even though now it's electronic. For research, I read, I read, and then I read some more.

I like what I wrote in my first memoir, *Phantom Limb*: "My husband says that I undertake research as a way to gain a measure of control. But I maintain that the coping mechanism, while useful, is secondary. Knowledge itself is the lure, the pursuit of it as if on a trail, ears perking, nose twitching, sniffing closer to the earth until I pick up first a strong scent, then the slow aromatic release of meaning." That's more than a description of research; it carries over into the whole writing process.

Many things trump research. When some piece of research-derived information sticks out, interrupts the story, forces a reader down another path, proclaims in the author's voice, "Aren't I smart?"—these are signals to drop those pieces of research. That type of information doesn't serve what a writer needs to tell. I put a lot of this extraneous material in the book before I learned what I had to take out. And then I took out too much! I took away valuable essay material—facts and speculation—so my story would flow better, which was a mistake. It actually flowed better when it became fuller, when I became more of a thinking and feeling person on the page, capable of moving nimbly among kinds of material.

AOR: *Writers like David Shields and Jonathan Lethem have popularized the idea that nonfiction necessarily requires liberty of the imagination, that there's fiction in all nonfiction. Did you have to make any leaps to fill in gaps of information? Did you have to take any literary liberties for the narrative's sake?*

JS: Much of *White Matter* takes place before I was born; how could I know what had happened? I couldn't, so I made it up. But I came up with a criterion for myself: scrupulous imagination. I knew these people, and I had a strong sense of what they might have said and done. I tried to be true to that criterion within my invention, and not wander off into flights of fancy.

The most potent examples are times I built on what was told to me. For example, my aunt Minna told me about her first love, Leon. Did I know that Sam, the man she eventually married, courted her by waiting while she put the cover on her Underwood typewriter so that he could walk her home each day? No. I made up that detail because it's consistent with what I know of Sam—that's the scrupulous part—because writing needs scene and action that show something defining about a character.

Any number of scenes in *White Matter* are like that, some about more important things than details within a scene. After the family gets together to decide whether Francie should have a lobotomy, I try to enter the minds of Minna, Pauline, and Francie. There's no way I could know what they were thinking—I'm definitely leaning on fictional devices—and yet it still feels scrupulous to me because I know who they were. I'm lucky to have had such a close relationship to my mother and aunts, to a family of storytellers. As an adult I used to listen to my mother talking about people who lived in her apartment building and think, *Chekhov*. I think that many more details and scenes were poured into me than into most children, for better and for worse to my psychological well-being, but definitely better for the making of a writer.

It's very tricky territory. The scene when the family decides Francie's fate is entirely a fiction—I have no idea how the decision was made, whether all together in Minna's apartment or in separate conversations that converged. While I was writing, I was aware, too, of a suspicious delight, a delicious sense of expanding abilities, putting all these characters into play in deft strokes. That said, is it radically *untrue*? If they hadn't all met in Minna's apartment, might they nonetheless have acted in the same ways, given the inevitabilities of their personalities? To that last, I say yes.

AOR: *This book is at times a memoir, a biographical family history, and a medical history. Which of those elements is most important and why? Whose story is this?*

JS: I resist separating out those elements because the work of this book was to do the opposite—to combine them into one story. Our lives play out at all those levels.

I was asked whose story this was along the way, with the implication that a reader has to find one person to identify with. I don't believe that. It should be possible for a reader to find parts of herself in many characters and care about what happens to all of them. I see the book as a prism—like those glass prisms dangling from my Aunt Jen's lamps, people show different facets of themselves and reflect one another.

I suppose it's my story, though, when all is said and done— but not exactly "me," I tried to make my voice into a character. I worked hard to find a voice for myself that a reader would engage with—someone interesting, whom readers wanted to follow to find out not only what would happen next but also what the writer would turn to next. I also wanted my voice to be someone who could see the humor in difficulty and could criticize herself. *White Matter* is in part the story of that voice and its struggle to survive.

AOR: *You spent much of your life separating yourself from the decisions your aunts and mother made for their siblings. Do you feel any regret about the impact that distancing had on your life?*

JS: That distancing was what helped me survive. Without it, my spirit would have been broken. So to regret it would mean that I regret living as a whole person. And that means living to tell my tales. This last is so important to *White Matter*. My cousins who were writers had to distance themselves—as did Tennessee Williams and Allen Ginsberg. Admittedly this is a pretty small sample because we are children of families with terrible mental illness, children of lobotomy. We escaped to write about it, not as observers but as people implicated in it. But the escape had to come first for the writer to come later.

Now to approach the question again: Do I feel any regret about distancing myself? The answer is yes. Distancing is a defensive stance, and that means I had to numb myself to what I'd left. There are kinds of closeness I wish I'd experienced and been able to give in those numbing years.

The book began with another sort of distancing—blame. I began thinking that my family had been evil when they decided on the lobotomies; that lobotomy was, simply, always the wrong thing to do even then; that Jen was to be blamed for insisting Francie move in with her; that Minna was to blame for not stopping Jen; and that my grandmother was to blame for loving Bennie in a way that did damage to her daughters.

At one level, the entire book is a story of drawing closer, of gaining perspective, of seeing many sides and many levels to the decisions my mother and aunts made. That kind of drawing closer is also a kind of honoring while remaining faithful to mistakes—to wrongs; to conditions of the times; to individual psychology; to the family's pity for Francie, so strong that drastic measures seemed a right course; to envy; to all the human dramas played out in my family. Had I been closer, I couldn't have seen things this way.

AOR: *Imagine Bennie and Francie were coming of age in today's world. You're not a psychiatrist, but what do you believe the likely treatments for their conditions might be? What better options were available at the time they received lobotomies?*

JS: I've come to believe something that at first shocked me: At the time, lobotomy was probably the best thing that could have happened to my uncle Bennie. Consider the alternative—there was none other than the insane asylums of that time, with their horrific conditions. Things are somewhat better now. Maybe not so much the pharmaceuticals that are now available—they may help as a path out of the worst symptoms of schizophrenia, but they've been called a chemical lobotomy because they dull people so severely that often the patient rebels, doesn't take the pills, and can spin off further into madness. When I say that things may be better, I'm thinking instead about new perspectives on the disease: encouragement for a person to see himself as more than his illness; cognitive therapies that show a person how to identify triggers and possibly avert a full-blown attack; books written by fellow sufferers from the inside that say "you are not alone"; and new support systems. None of it is a cure, but it's better, and perhaps some combination of these newer resources might have helped Bennie.

And I've also come to believe that Francie's lobotomy was a tragedy—that's one of the main threads in *White Matter*, how so many different things came together to destroy her. If she were alive now, I think she might have been helped by new medications for depression. She was living with such acute trauma that her serotonin levels had to have been close to empty. Perhaps if those levels could have been built back up, she might have found it easier to cope. And if none of the new medications worked, then perhaps she could have been helped by a cingulotomy. Yes, a brain surgery, but one infinitely more precise that has a decent track record of lifting acute depressions. But I don't fool myself—these are terrible illnesses that require intensive treatments.

AOR: *What effect do you think publishing this book will have on your family?*

JS: I worried about this for years—that I'd hurt someone. Then, because the book took so long, they all died. I'm standing alone on this one.

With *Phantom Limb*, my earlier memoir, I worried, and I was right to do so. One relative said she'd cautioned another relative not to be upset by my book—that even though it wasn't the way she remembered it, she had to understand I was constructing a story, not trying to get everything *right*. I was so relieved. Later on I heard she'd actually said the opposite—that I had betrayed the family.

I also tried fooling myself. I tried giving one person uncharacteristic clothes, thinking she wouldn't recognize herself. But the deeper stuff is always recognizable.

One of the most important things to me as a writer is the need—the human necessity—to feel. In *Phantom Limb*, I juxtaposed my mother's loss of her leg and the phantom limb pain she felt —a pain in a body part that wasn't there—with the case of a woman, Madame I, as she is known in early twentieth-century neurological literature, who could feel nothing, even though the doctors could find no organic cause. Without feeling, she had no sense of who she was, no memories that could sustain themselves and her over time. Madame I was my mother's opposite. At the end of *Phantom Limb*, I imagine the two women meeting up in the Bois de Bologne, able to walk together now that Madame I's ability to feel has been restored. But then Madame I falls to the ground and feels a stab of acute pain. Later, when she recovers, my mother asks her whether remembering is worth it if it brings pain. She answers tartly that the question is nonsense, and ends by saying, "I can hear my children at last." In other words, the memory of what she loves—the feeling of love—is more essential to her than enduring physical pain. I wouldn't want to put this to the test of torture, but for most of us in more ordinary situations I believe that feeling is essential. And in *White Matter*, this—the capacity to feel—is what was taken from Bennie and Francie. That's what white matter is—it's the brain's switchboard between the limbic system and the prefrontal lobes, between thinking and feeling. It's what is cut in a lobotomy. Whether it was necessary is another story—in fact, it's the story of the book.

AOR: *Early in* White Matter, *your aunt Pauline asked you why you were writing this book. Do you have an answer to her question?*

JS: I could answer this question in abstract ways: to find meaning in chaos; to create a structure for complexity; etc. But these are general reasons.

An interviewer once asked the great French filmmaker Jean Vigo, "Why do you keep making films?" He replied that he had an itch, so he had to keep scratching it.

In *White Matter*, one big itch was, "How could my relatives have done this terrible thing?" Another itch was, "I thought they were good people but they weren't—or were they?" Those were the itches that didn't let up. I had to go on scratching.

Perhaps it's because I majored in philosophy and I don't like to let questions dangle, perhaps too because I belong to what I call "the meaning generation"—adults brought up on the writing of Holocaust survivors such as Viktor Frankl, who wrote *Man's Search for Meaning*—that I believe meaning matters.

I had wondered whether my relatives were the good, kind people I had always thought them to be. But nothing is ever one thing. We need a human vision that encompasses all the dimensions of the human being. We need to unite compassion with a moral vision that includes complexity. We can choose to understand knowledge as a lifelong venture without final answers.

Along the way, writing this book, I felt the sting of moral outrage. For good reason. But outrage only goes so far. It's awfully black and white. About Bennie, Minna had asked, "What if it doesn't work?" My mother added the original cost/benefit question: "What do you think will happen if we don't do it?" What if one has to face the excruciating necessity of choice without that vaunted knowledge? Pauline, her skepticism especially aroused by anything she saw as possibly falling under Minna's control, asked about Francie, "How do we know?" My mother said, "You have to trust somebody." In the end, you do.

AOR: *Now that this book is done, what projects excite you? Are you working on something?*

JS: I've always wanted to write a trilogy that combines my life and the life of my family with broader themes, especially those of science.

I'm two-thirds along the way. The first book is *Phantom Limb*. The second book is this one. Now I want to write the third. It's clear to me what I have to do. The first one began because I needed to know about my mother's phantom limb syndrome so that I could help her. This book began because a friend who had read the first book said, "Now I want to know about the sisters."

Now friends and readers have said, "It's your turn. I want to know about the breadth and depth of your own life." I have a file full of stories I've written toward this new book under the working title "Gypsy Curiosa," which is a type of rose whose colors become more intense as it ages.

The writerly problem I'm facing is that I haven't yet found my metaphor, my structuring principle that can open the book up to encompass more than myself. I can't really write without that. I was able to write *Phantom Limb* when I realized the condition of experiencing something no longer there as though it's still there is actually the human condition—we've all lost something that remains present even though it's absent. It's more than just an idea about memory. If it had been only that, it would have been just a literary fancy. But I did a lot of research in neurology and discovered that phantom limb is the neurological circuitry in the brain carrying on as it always has, even in the absence of the limb. So it's more than the notion of memory; it's built into our very being and is continuity itself.

With *White Matter*, the themes are so strong—the way love is intertwined with damage, the impossibility of knowing anything for certain but having to take action nonetheless—that it may seem difficult to see the structure of metaphor that lies under those themes. But it's there. It begins with the fact that a lobotomy leaves a person indifferent. The contrast with indifference—a widespread condition in modern life—is what makes lobotomy, a long-discredited operation, press on in our present moment. But an equal piece of the metaphor is the very opposite of indifference,

and that's feeling. The story of my relatives and myself is supported by stakes that have deeper meaning: Do we live with indifference, or do we allow feeling in for better and for worse?

In addition to the third book in the trilogy, I'm working on
a book of my photographs. Taking photographs is another way of
being, very different from what I call the furrowed brow of writing.
It's the most highly refined form of play that I know. For this book,
Overspilling World, I'm playing with juxtapositions, image beside
image, and image combined with text.

AOR: *What impact do you hope* White Matter *has on its readers?*

JS: I've always wanted to move people, to move their hearts so
they'll be emotionally changed by reading this book, to move them
into an awareness of things that need to be changed, and to move
them into a greater appreciation of complexity and ambiguities.

I also hope *White Matter* will contribute to a conversation
on what Nicholas Kristof has called "the systematically neglected
issue of mental health." As he writes, "All across America and the
world, families struggle with these issues, but people are more
likely to cry quietly in bed than speak out." I hope my family's story
will rouse more people to speak out.

Discussion questions

1. The author, as a child, lived in a situation where things were hidden—her family's life seemed normal on the surface, but extreme things were happening underneath. The book shows a child trying to make sense of this. Is covering up, pretending to be normal, a common experience?

2. The author has to imagine scenes before she was born; she tells you at the beginning that she has decided upon a strategy she calls "scrupulous imagination." Do you think that such a thing is possible?

3. What are the risks of making things up? In memoir does a reader need exact truths, or is there an understanding between writer and reader that memoir is always a construct? Especially in a book such as *White Matter* that combines genres—memoir, essay, and story?

4. At one point, Minna's "well of pity went dry"—what happens when people reach their limits?

5. Did you think Minna was right when she didn't want Francie to see Harry at the end of his life? When Helen did? Where does compassion lie—with protecting people, or with giving them a chance to make their own decisions even if they will lead to suffering?

6. Could Francie have been saved if she hadn't had the lobotomy? Might the passage of time, as Pauline says, have helped?

Might getting away from the family, as the author suggests, have helped? Or was her downfall inevitable?

7. What would you have done if faced with the decision about Bennie's treatment?

8. What would you have done fifteen years later, at the time of the decision for Francie's treatment?

9. What did you think when Janet felt sad at Walter Freeman's death? Was that sudden sadness, which surprised her, understandable to you after all the damage he had done?

10. Is there any other practice—medical or otherwise—where good intentions become mixed with personal motivations to dire effect?

11. Should medical professionals be trained to have less of a sense of entitlement? To have greater empathy with their patients?

12. Have you ever blamed people and then felt you were too harsh? Have you ever tried to swing in the other direction, to let people off the hook because you wanted to be seen as nice? What do you think of the author's desire to find a place between those poles?

13. How is it that good people can do bad things? Does this echo other situations? What has to be taken into account for something to be considered bad?

14. Have there been situations in your own experience that could not be made better by amassing more information?

15. Each of the sisters handles the aftermath of the tragedies in her own way: Minna by reflecting on it; Jen by avoiding it; Helen by living in the present. What do you think of these strategies for getting on with one's life?

16. "It was the times"—is that a good excuse for what happened to Bennie and Francie? Where does individual morality come into play?